READY, SET, SCALE

Scaling Your Business Without Losing Your
Soul

BY STEPHEN ADELÉ AND ZACH LEWIS

READY FOR SCALING, DENVER, CO

Justin,

Here's to your scaling successes!

TEAM AGOGE

Ready Set Scale – Scaling Your Business Without Losing Your Soul / by Stephen Adelé and Zach Lewis – Denver, CO: Ready for Scaling Inc, 2024
p. cm.

ISBN: 9 781304 213952 (Hardcover)
ISBN: 9 781304 213969 (Softcover)

Published by Ready for Scaling Inc.
951 20th St #104
Denver, CO 80201

www.readyforscaling.com

Printed in the United States of America

Publisher's Cataloging-in-Publication Data
Adelé, Stephen, 1971

Cover design by Jhonny at Digital Art on DesignCrowd.com
Edited by Sue Mosebar

Dedication and Inspiration

To all the visionary entrepreneurs who have come before us: you embody the indomitable American spirit and exemplify the power of a capitalist system that has fostered unparalleled opportunities and advancements. Your courage, innovation, and unwavering pursuit of dreams have forged a path for countless others to follow.

We must remember that a system, like capitalism, is only as robust as the individuals who operate within it. For our societal structures to continue evolving and improving, each of us must strive for continuous self-improvement and hold ourselves accountable. This book is dedicated to democratizing the journey of scaling, empowering more noble-hearted and ambitious individuals to ascend to greatness and make a lasting, positive impact on the world.

Let us move forward together, creating a future where opportunity and success are within reach for all, propelled by individuals who embody integrity, perseverance, and a steadfast commitment to bettering themselves and the systems they work within.

READY, SET, SCALE

CONTENTS

PART THREE: Scaling Sustainably

Preface

WHAT STARTED IT ALL

"Built to Scale. Built to Sell."

These were the first words I uttered during our initial meeting in October 2016. The four of us gathered for dinner at a taproom restaurant in Broomfield, Colorado, to discuss our next business venture. This time, we were determined to do things differently. We aimed to build a business with the end in mind, creating a company that was built to scale and, ultimately, built to sell.

The meeting felt almost serendipitous. Each of us had just concluded our previous business endeavors, and we were searching for the next opportunity. As we discussed our future plans, we envisioned ideal scenarios and explored the latest trends in direct-to-consumer selling, online shopping, and the rapid rise of new consumer goods brands. We unanimously agreed on entering the third-party logistics order fulfillment sector. The timing was perfect given the trends, but more importantly, we saw an industry ripe for disruption.

Three months later, we signed a lease on a 105,000-square-foot warehouse in Denver, Colorado, and QuickBox, our third-party order fulfillment company, was born. I still remember standing in that vast, empty space, scratching my head, and wondering, "How long will it take us to fill this place?"

From that moment, I knew this venture would be different. It represented the culmination of everything I had learned about scaling from my previous three companies.

This time, I had the privilege of doing it alongside partners who were incredibly talented and just as passionate about our opportunity. Despite having no industry experience and zero outside capital, at the helm of QuickBox as its CEO, I held onto an unwavering belief that we could apply the principles of scaling—*the very principles you're about to learn*—and achieve our desired outcome.

Fast forward four years, and we earned a spot on the Inc. 500 list of fastest-growing companies in America for three consecutive years. We became finalists for EY's prestigious Entrepreneur of the Year award, serviced hundreds of explosive consumer goods brands, employed over 500 people, surpassed $100 million in revenues, and ultimately sold the company to a private equity fund.

Interestingly, though, about three-quarters of the way through this journey, something unexpected happened. We were already scaling at warp speed, but this event would propel us to unprecedented levels of growth. Quite frankly, it was uncharted territory. It would test every one of our scaling principles and force us to do everything possible to maintain our company's soul and preserve our personal sanity.

The date was March 13, 2020: a day that remains as vivid in my memory as yesterday. And a day, I'm certain, that has etched itself into the consciousness of nearly every American. Mostly because of the unforeseen challenges and opportunities it was about to present to all of us.

Like any other morning, my routine began with a keen glance at the iQ data report for our third-party order fulfillment center, QuickBox. However, this was no ordinary day. The numbers before me painted an unprecedented picture: our daily order volume had not just doubled but tripled and, for some clients, even quadrupled *overnight*.

The reason behind this surge? A statewide shelter-at-home order announced by Colorado Governor Polis, mirroring actions taken across the nation in response to the emerging global crisis. This mandate effectively shuttered physical retail spaces, propelling consumers toward online shopping and, inadvertently, creating a windfall for direct-to-consumer e-commerce companies.

Without notice, QuickBox found itself squarely at the epicenter of this unexpected boon. Specializing in serving direct-to-consumer e-commerce brands, we were already navigating the complexities of scaling at a breakneck pace, with year-over-year growth exceeding 400 percent. Yet, the shelter order forced us into uncharted territory, necessitating an immediate quadrupling of our incoming order volume to keep pace with demand. The realization hit swiftly, and with it, the enormity of the task ahead.

I did the math, understanding the implications of this surge, and promptly called up our ownership group. The message was clear and urgent: we needed to hire 500 new team members. *Today.*

The days, weeks, and months that followed were a whirlwind of activity, decision-making, and relentless pursuit of solutions. We fondly referred to these high-pressure, high-reward situations as "champagne problems." It wasn't quite as challenging as changing engines on a flying plane; it was more like ensuring the wheels stayed firmly on the bus as we navigated through the steep, winding road of this unprecedented scaling opportunity.

You see, I had built, scaled, and sold three other companies before QuickBox. In other words, this wasn't my first rodeo. But this one was different. It was wildly complex. It was unexpected. This period of intense growth served as a crucible, stress-testing every process, system, and the collective intellect and resilience of our team. It was a testament to the robustness of the foundational truths in scaling I had come to rely on over the years, even as it laid bare the areas in need of refinement and strengthening.

It was profoundly rewarding to make it through this scaling period, especially during a time of such uncertainty. But, it was most rewarding to see the tried-and-true principles I had created for scaling put into effect. Principles that worked marvelously well. So well, we would break through the $100-million mark after only four years since QuickBox's inception. It was quite an extraordinary time, to say the least.

This experience, transformative in its intensity and scope, set the stage for a pivotal meeting that would further shape my journey in entrepreneurship and this book. It was during this period of reflection and crystallization of lessons learned that I converged paths with Zach Lewis.

Our initial interactions took place against the backdrop of academic pursuit at the University of Denver, where we collaborated on several projects. I was immediately struck by Zach's extraordinary acumen for business and his ability to translate the rigorous discipline, strategic foresight, and adaptability cultivated during his time as a US Navy SEAL to the challenges and opportunities of the business world. Zach brought to the table a unique set of skills and complementary perspectives, honed in environments where stakes transcended the financial and ventured into the realm of life and death.

Our partnership evolved naturally, born out of mutual respect and a shared vision for applying our collective experiences, and we would eventually team up to take our collective learnings and consult and guide other businesses. This book, co-authored with Zach, is a culmination of our prior experiences, insights, and the lessons we've garnered along the way in our unique journeys. It's a narrative about scaling your company without losing your soul, about turning challenges into opportunities, and ultimately, about the transformative power of entrepreneurship when guided by values, a grander vision, and a proven framework that, when applied, has the ability to unlock exponential growth in your business.

Welcome to our story, which is about to become your story—a journey of growth, learning, and the meaningful pursuit of scaling.

An Introduction:

THE ART AND HEART OF SCALING

Make no mistake, few journeys are as exhilarating, challenging, and transformative as scaling a business. From the spark of an idea to its execution, each step you've taken has led you to this pivotal moment. You're not just looking to grow; you're aiming to soar. To scale your business to an entirely new level.

Why Scale, and Why Now?

In this dynamic, digital age, standing still can often feel like moving backward. Scaling isn't merely a path to greater revenues or wider recognition. It's an ambitious quest to amplify your impact, to reach more people, and to ensure your business not only survives but sustainably thrives—leaving a legacy you can be proud of. And, if done right, provide you with a treasure chest of key learnings and a bank account full of money. However, scaling is not just about quantitative growth. It's about qualitative evolution. It's about being mindful of:

- How you expand your venture without losing sight of its core values.
- How you maintain the essence and ethos that set you apart.
- How to manage everything along the way, without losing your sh*t!
- In essence, how you scale your company, *without* losing your soul.

Herein lies the true challenge: preserving your business's heart and soul even as you expand its footprint at warp speed. There are countless tales of companies that, in their quest for growth, lost their distinct identity or strayed from their foundational principles, or worse, imploded and died.

Companies like EAS (Experimental & Applied Sciences), the first company I worked for after college. When we sold to Abbott Laboratories in 2005 for $320 million, we were generating over $200 million in sales. We also had a robust and unique culture that quickly crumbled after the new owners presided.

Sadly, in 2018, Abbott closed the doors on EAS, mainly because the principal players had failed to adjust their strategy to a changing market. The reign of what had once been the largest sports nutrition brand in the world came to a crushing end.

Or Sol Cuisine, Canada's oldest plant-based protein company. They sold to PlantPlus Foods in 2022 for $125 million. Then, due to leadership issues and a lack of continued innovation, eroding the essence of the company's originating values, it found itself closing its doors a mere two years later.

Another example that comes to mind is a past fulfillment client of ours at QuickBox, called LadyBoss. This was a growing weight-loss supplement brand, led by a vibrant set of co-founders who had surpassed $25 million in online sales within just a few years after starting the company. The company was sure to soar to the $100 million mark. Then, in a bizarre twist of operational missteps and a surprising internal cultural backlash, the business shut down a year later.

All of these remarkable stories of business deaths were preventable.

This book is intended to be your guide to ensure your scaling story is different. *Much different.*

Introducing a Guiding, Principles-Centered Path

At the heart of this book is a proven framework, crafted through real-world experiences, dedicated to helping businesses like yours scale rapidly without losing their (or your) essence. This isn't just a collection of theories or growth hacks; it's a roadmap, filled with actionable insights, practical strategies, interactive tools, and a deep understanding of the purposeful side of scaling.

As we explore these pages together, you'll encounter invaluable lessons, interspersed with captivating stories, cautionary tales, and, where appropriate, a dash of humility to enlighten the journey.

The mission… To equip you to not just grow your business but *truly* scale it, while staying true to its core values.

So, What Awaits You?

By the conclusion of our journey, you will:
- Grasp the intricacies and importance of scaling in the modern entrepreneurial landscape.
- Be armed with a battle-tested, proven framework to guide your scaling business venture.
- Learn to use a set of custom tools we've developed to help implement and optimize each of the phases of scaling (tools I desperately wished I'd had earlier in my entrepreneurial journey).
- Identify the constraints within your business and intimately understand how they'll hold back your ability to scale (or perhaps already are) and discover how to systematically unlock them.

- Acquire deep insights on how to retain and even strengthen your company's cultural spirit amid rapid growth.
- Build your IQ surrounding business, and equally importantly, stack the deck in favor of the emotional fortitude you'll need to persist and achieve scale.
- Benefit from a rich array of case study examples, anecdotes, and years of practical wisdom to bring relevance to your scaling journey.

Let's face it: scaling a venture is no small feat. But with the right tools, a clear vision, unwavering passion, hard work, and Zach and me as your guides (think of us as your personal Sherpas, climbing the treacherous scaling mountain alongside you), it's a challenge worth taking on. And frankly, it's unlike *anything* you've ever experienced.

So, turn the page, and let's prepare to embark on a transformative expedition together.

Are you ready to scale without losing your soul?

PART ONE:

On Scaling

.

Chapter 1

Scaling vs. Growing – Charting the Right Path to Massive Expansion

In the lexicon of business musings, "growth" and "scaling" are often used interchangeably, like distant cousins frequently mistaken for twins. Yet, understanding the nuanced differences between them is not just academic—it's critical for any entrepreneur aiming to steer their venture beyond the horizons of success without losing their sanity or, worse, their soul.

Let's take a minute to demystify these concepts, highlight their differences, and spotlight the unique characteristics of scaling and the paramount importance in the entrepreneurial quest for the idealistic business mantra: "built to scale."

Growth vs. Scaling: Unraveling the Key Distinctions

For our purposes, we'll need to draw a clear distinction between two
critical concepts in business growth and scaling.

Growth, in its truest sense, is characterized by the increase in a company's resources and revenues at a similar rate. It's a straightforward
expansion strategy where adding resources, such as capital, workforce, and technology, directly contributes to increasing revenue.
This linear relationship between investment and output is essential
for the initial stages, but it becomes *unsustainable* for long-term
prosperity without significant capital infusion or radicalization of its
culture—surrounding performance and expected output by the individual contributors in the company.

Scaling, in contrast, focuses on increasing revenue *without* a proportional increase in resources or costs. It's about enhancing operational efficiency and productivity to achieve exponential growth. A
company that scales successfully can serve *more* customers and generate *more* revenue with relatively fewer cost increases. This involves optimizing the existing operations to improve output without
equivalently expanding resource base.

Allow me to emphasize that scaling is the strategic amplification of
a company's capabilities and resources to achieve growth that out-
strips the incremental costs typically associated with expansion.

And this, my entrepreneurial friend, is how you maximize the value of your enterprise.

So, what exactly do we mean by "scaling" when it comes to business? Imagine you've just baked the most delicious protein bar in your small oven at home. Your friends love it, and they want more! As do your neighbors. Someone gives one to the manager of the grocery store in town, and they want to stock it for their shoppers. Now, if you were to merely "grow," you'd make protein bar after bar, night and day, exhausting yourself and your resources. If you worked feverishly in your business, you might grow annual revenues by 10, 15, or even 20 percent.

But to "scale"? That's when you revamp your kitchen or outsource your bakery needs altogether, so you can produce thousands of protein bars for the same effort as making the first delicious bar. In this scenario, working just as hard, but on the business rather than baking, you could scale revenues at 100, 200, or even 1,000 percent—while barely increasing your operating expenditures.

In essence, scaling is about enhancing your capacity to deliver more without proportionally increasing your resources. It isn't just about growing bigger. It's about growing smarter and stronger and, as a result, faster. In business speak, it's worth repeating: *scaling is a company's capability to increase its output, revenue, or impact without a direct linear increase in its resources or costs.* In essence, it's supercharged growth with elements of operational elegance and incredibly well-orchestrated efficiency to prevent cash burn-through and resource burnout.

Whereas an inefficient (or unsustainable) business, on the other hand, exhausts its resources—including cash and people—as it tries to grow more rapidly. Unless reined in, the company can burn through cash and energy until it reaches a financial crisis or flat-out burnout. Living in this high-stress state over long periods diminishes passion, drains the soul, and can lead to poor decision-making. Plus, it rarely ends in sustainable revenue growth.

Scaling Done Right: A Few Recent Case Studies

Many companies, which you're likely already familiar with (and use), exemplify the principles of successful scaling more recently. For instance, Airbnb leveraged technology to disrupt the traditional hospitality industry, connecting hosts and travelers worldwide without the need to own a single piece of property. This platform model enabled Airbnb to scale rapidly with relatively low incremental costs. Now, as of this writing, Airbnb's market capitalization (enterprise value of a publicly traded company) is $102 billion. Compare that to the hotel industry leaders—Hyatt, Marriott, and Hilton—with a *combined* market capitalization of barely $40 billion!

Similarly, Dropbox excelled in scaling by focusing on systematization and automation. By creating a product that seamlessly integrated with users' existing workflows that took users from an offline world of paper to an online world of storing their documents "in the cloud," Dropbox could scale its service without a proportional increase in support staff or infrastructure. Co-founded in 2007 and led by Drew Houston, Dropbox now serves over 700 million registered users and is valued at $8 billion!

"Netflix and Chill" may have emerged from social media musings, but Netflix's evolution from a DVD mail-order rental service to a global streaming powerhouse is another masterclass in scaling. Through strategic investments in content and technology and always staying one giant step ahead of the previous, antiquated ways of serving up and watching movies at home, Netflix was able to grow its subscriber base and revenue exponentially without a corresponding increase in marginal costs per subscriber. Netflix is now valued at a staggering $272 billion!

For a more humble example, let's look at my most recent venture, QuickBox, where I led the company to $100 million in revenues in under five years. This type of scaling was only possible with an incredibly talented co-founder and executive leadership team, a clear and compelling business strategy, superior process automation, and our ability to fund growth through a surplus of negative cash conversion cycles. While we weren't classified as a "unicorn"—an enterprise valued at over a billion dollars—we were able to sell the company to a private equity firm for a healthy sum! (We'll provide a more in-depth case study on QuickBox later on and throughout the chapters.)

Knowing how to scale, though, isn't just for titans. It's for every entrepreneur building a small, medium, or large-scale enterprise who dreams of making a difference and providing a massive impact, like you. Starting a business takes a leap of faith. Sure, there is boundless potential, evidenced by the score of companies that not only grow year over year but scale at a growth trajectory like those just mentioned. Make no mistake, there are also plenty of risks, evidenced by the graveyard of businesses that close their doors even after years of devoting time and dedication to building their legacy.

Since 2007, 23 percent of startups didn't make it to year two. After five years, 54 percent had succumbed to various pressures and folded. And, by year ten, 67 percent had closed their doors for good. By the fifteenth year, a mere 25 percent of the companies started that year were still in existence.

These trends have remained consistent over various cyclical times, which speaks to internal factors rather than external, like the 2008 economic crisis, as the primary drivers leading to the death of the businesses.

One study (by Jessie Hagen at U.S. Bank) found 82 percent of business owners cite cash flow issues as the primary reason they were unable to succeed over the long term. *We would argue, though, that cash flow problems are merely the last grain of sand to sink the ship*—and there were systemic issues constraining their growth potential that could have likely been seen (and solved) further ahead of time to prevent their demise.

It's safe to say, anyone in business today understands the market is an ever-evolving beast. With technological advancements and changing consumer behavior, being stationary is akin to moving backward.

Businesses that master scaling are the ones that stay ahead of the curve, dictating trends rather than just following them, thus keeping the doors open, even when the uncontrollable macro forces and headwinds turn turbulent.

Scaling is more than a business buzzword. Companies that scale effectively don't just lead the market; they define and dominate it. They anticipate trends, set benchmarks, and create new roadmaps.

Holding onto Your Soul as You Scale Your Business

Let's lean in for a moment to a softer but just as important topic. In the pursuit of greatness, it's easy to get lost. Bigger numbers, a wider reach, and market dominance can be dazzling. So, as you set your eyes on distant and vast horizons, there's something you must hold close, almost sacred: The soul of your company.

The stresses and challenges business leaders face, that we face as entrepreneurs, can be (and are) immense. They often determine the course of your company. Scaling without a soul is like a ship without a compass. You might move fast, but it's all too easy to lose your way.

But here's the good news. It's not only possible to scale while retaining your company's core values; it's imperative. As an entrepreneur, you aren't just a decision-maker. You're the guardian of your company's values. You're the driving force behind its vision.

Your engagement and intense focus are infectious, motivating the entire organization. It's what builds up your company culture in a positive way.

Maintaining your original passion and values, though, isn't just inspirational; it's strategic. They guide decision-making, foster loyalty among customers, and attract like-minded talent who resonate with your principles. A true win-win-win, as we like to say. And it's the sole reason it's vitally important that we remain mindful of staying true to our essence as we scale.

At The Heart of Scaling

Scaling is part art form and part empirical science, requiring a unique blend of strategic foresight, operational efficiency, and cultural integrity. It's about building a business that can not only with-stand the trials of expansion but thrive in them, preserving its essence while reaching new heights of success.

As we continue on this journey, remember that scaling is not an end-point but a process, a continuous quest for efficiency and impact. By embracing our principles of scaling, you can guide your business through the uncharted territory of rapid expansion, ensuring that as it grows faster and more steeply, it does so not just in size but in strength and spirit as well.

Chapter 2

The Foreseen (and Unknown)
Problems of Scaling

In the journey of entrepreneurship, scaling a business is an endeavor filled with contrasts—it's as rewarding as it is challenging, as exciting as it is daunting. This phase, while rich with opportunities and excitement, is also laced with hurdles that often aren't apparent until you're faced with them.

As someone who has navigated the turbulent waters of scaling several times—in my own companies and with many consulting clients—we've come to understand the nuances of these challenges intimately.

Lest we forget, this book is written for you, the entrepreneur... CEO... business owner... executive leader... who has tasted the sweet victory of initial success. Maybe you've reached your first million... or ten or twenty-five million, but now you find yourself in unfamiliar territory. The path forward isn't as clear.

Before we dive into our principles for scaling, let's take a moment to truly connect with the challenges at hand—the problems you may be experiencing with your business that are not only common but deeply misunderstood.

We've found there are three distinct challenges we face while growing a business. And before we embark on your scaling journey, it's beneficial to see if one or all of them apply to you:

Challenge #1: Reevaluating the Solo Journey

The belief in the strength of our independence, the notion that we can and should tackle every challenge and run every piece of our business on our own, is a trait many entrepreneurs, including myself, share. This rugged individualism is a double-edged sword: It can be both the driving force behind our initial successes and a barrier to further growth.

The reluctance to seek help, often rooted in a fear of exposing vulnerabilities, is a sentiment I know all too well. In fact, looking back, I'd be remiss if I didn't admit that was one of my greatest regrets during my early entrepreneurial pursuits. That is, I let my "I can do it all myself; I don't need any help" ego get in the way of listening to those more experienced business mentors and advisors. Yet, realizing that you're not alone in feeling this way is a powerful acknowledgment. It's a shared experience among many who have embarked on the path to scaling. But, letting this attitude continue to reign, especially when you're about to enter hypergrowth mode, is only going to become a punitive, rate-limiting factor to your growth and ultimate scaling success.

Challenge #2: Facing the Agonizing Revenue Plateau

There comes a point when growth unexpectedly stalls—maybe you reached the $1 million, $10 million, or $25 million revenue point, and the momentum that once propelled your business forward seems to have vanished into thin air. It feels like you're banging your head against the ceiling and wondering why you can't seem to break through.

This plateau can be bewildering, leaving you questioning every decision and strategy that previously brought about success this far. It's a scenario I'm all too familiar with. What's happened? Looking in hindsight, it's clear to me the strategies and work ethic that served us well suddenly become ineffective, signaling a need for change without a clear direction. In response, you lean in further—working harder and longer, only to find yourself coming up short, exhausted, and feeling more burned out than ever.

This experience is far from unique. In fact, it's typically a rite of passage for many business owners seeking to scale. In working with our clients, it's by far the number one reason they come to us. Asking, "How do I break through this ceiling and spur growth in my business again?" to share the burden is the first step to overcoming it.

Challenge #3: Navigating the Hidden Complexities of Growth

I'm sure you've heard the expression, "You don't know what you don't know!" As cliche as it sounds, there is a foundational truth in these words, especially as you're about to embark on a scaling journey. As your business expands, it unveils a layer of internal-derived complexities that were previously hidden—operational, legal, financial, and cultural challenges that begin to surface. It's called entropy. These challenges, invisible during the early hustle, become significant constraints as you scale. In most situations, you may not even be aware of the landmines that lie ahead that can derail even the best-laid plans.

I've felt the frustration myself, nearly watching my business crumble from the inside (despite incredible revenue growth) and putting me just inches away from filing bankruptcy.

Surprised by hitting unexpected operational roadblocks... system failures, structural incongruencies, outdated business strategies, the stress of financial constraints tightening their grip, and the pain of a culture that, once joyful and fun, unknowingly becomes toxic and struggles to keep pace with hypergrowth.

Recognizing these growing pains, *before they happen*, is not only important, it's imperative. As is understanding that they are a common part of the scaling journey that must be avoided at all costs. For emphasis, let me say that again: identifying these growing pains *before* they hit you over the head is imperative to pave the way to scaling success.

However, if you've already encountered these growing pains and are currently dealing with them, it's important to step back and reassess the situation. And if stuck, try looking at the challenge with a fresh perspective, utilizing our principled framework. This approach will not only provide you with new insights and ways to move forward but also enable you to navigate through these obstacles more effectively and get back on the path to scaling success.

Finding Common Ground

As we stand at the precipice of delving deeper into these challenges, remember that identifying them is the precursor to navigating through them. Identifying where you're at with them should not just serve as an overview of the struggles to sustain breakneck growth but an empathetic acknowledgment of the journey we're about to embark on. I've walked in your shoes and felt the uncertainty, the frustration, the pain, and the isolation that can come with building a business. But through these shared experiences, my hope is we will find common ground and a starting point for our transformative journey ahead.

Chapter 3

The Prerequisites to Scaling: Laying the Groundwork for Exponential Growth

Before we embark on the journey of scaling your business, we first need to understand the underlying fundamentals that support sustainable growth, as they are as important as the principles of scaling themselves. Just as a skyscraper requires a strong foundation to withstand the forces of nature, a business needs a solid base to manage the pressures of scaling.

At Ready-for-Scaling (our consulting firm), before we engage with a client, we seek to uncover three key elements within the business, which are characterized by answering these questions:

First, *has the company met the fundamental "scaling prereq-uisites"?*

Next, *what are the constraints holding the company back from scaling?*

And finally, *does the leader have the capacity and willing-ness to endure the process of scaling?*

(The answers to these questions help us to determine a com-pany's "scale-readiness.")

Before we begin the process of scaling, we need to ensure the groundwork—i.e., a solid foundation—is in place. This foundation is non-negotiable. And so, we've found the answers to these ques-tions help to better set the stage to allow us to determine if a com-pany and its leader are qualified and prepared to take on the monu-mental task of scaling.

We call this the "Golden Trio."

Central to the "Golden Trio" are the scaling prerequisites, followed by the company's internal audit, and finally, the leader's emotional scale-readiness. As we explore the "Golden Trio" and the nuances of personal readiness, let this chapter act as a guide, highlighting the indispensable elements for scaling success and encouraging intro-spection on your readiness for the journey ahead.

Aligning these prerequisites with your values and goals sets a foundation for not just a profitable venture but a fulfilling scaling journey.

The Essential Prerequisites to Scaling

Let's first delve into each of the essential prerequisites for scaling your business effectively, ensuring your growth is not only rapid but also sustainable and aligned with your core values.

Prerequisite #1: $1 Million Financial Milestone

Achieving $1 million in trailing twelve months (TTM) revenue is often celebrated as a significant milestone for startups, and rightly so. This benchmark is a robust indicator of initial market validation. It is a testament that your product or service has moved beyond the early adopters and has begun to resonate with a broader market segment. In addition, reaching this milestone also indicates your ability to solve the initial challenges that come with starting a business, often referred to as "startup kinks."

These early "startup" phase challenges can range from identifying the right roles for the limited staff, setting up skeleton operations, and establishing initial product or service positioning. Overcoming these challenges, which is often indicative of reaching $1 million in TTM revenue, signifies you are not merely capturing revenues but also have vetted out a business model that has been tested and proven in the real market.

Prerequisite #2: Product-Market Fit

Product-market fit is achieved when your company's product or service meets strong market demand, which is typically evidenced by high user retention (repeat purchase) rates, organic growth through word-of-mouth, resilient customer loyalty despite competition, and reasonable customer acquisition costs.

This crucial alignment signifies that the product or service not only attracts but also satisfactorily retains its user base, suggesting an ideal harmony between what's offered and what the market desires. In essence, you solve a problem, and you do it well.

To assess and leverage your product-market fit, we typically look for and monitor key metrics, such as user feedback on various social media platforms, online reviews, Net Promoter Scores (NPS), customer acquisition costs, and repeat purchase patterns. Once an initial product-market fit has been established, we find the company is more readily able to shift to expanding market reach in its serviceable market and is better apt to continuously enhance the product or service based on user data and feedback, which sets the stage for sustainable growth and expansion.

Prerequisite #3: A Predictable Customer Attraction Model

Scaling requires more than just an influx of new customers; it necessitates a sustainable model that not only attracts but also retains customers. In the digital age, where customer loyalty is fleeting, and brands can get canceled with the click of a button, the ability to keep your customers coming back is a testament to the effectiveness of your brand's affinity, mainly due to its customer-activation model.

A predictable customer-attraction model, whether you're selling a product or service, is akin to a well-oiled machine that operates efficiently at every stage of the customer journey. From the initial awareness stage through purchase and post-purchase support to the online reviews posted by your customers and word-of-mouth to their circle of influence, every interaction is an opportunity to solidify your relationship with your customer. This model isn't just about marketing strategies or sales funnel hacks. It's about understanding whether your company has developed a holistic brand experience that resonates with customers on a fundamental level, ensuring they not only love your product but also feel valued and part of your community.

The Scale-Ready Self-Assessment: Uncovering Constraints

In the world of business, decisions based on data and introspection often lead to more predictable and positive outcomes. We've found that most entrepreneurs who claim they are ready to scale their companies aren't really sure if the company is actually able to scale. As the saying goes, "What gets measured gets managed (and usually what gets done)." And before embarking on the ambitious journey of scaling, it's critical to know exactly where you stand.

This is where the "Scale-Ready Self-Assessment" comes in.

The Scale Ready Self-Assessment is a pivotal framework we've designed to assess and prepare your business for substantial growth. This proprietary tool is akin to a comprehensive health check-up for your business, meticulously crafted over years of working intimately with companies to illuminate the venture's scalability and readiness for rapid, sustainable expansion. Think of it as a business diagnostic tool.

The Scale Ready Self-Assessment is a comprehensive survey that systematically evaluates key aspects of your business that are crucial to know, *before* attempting to scale. These dimensions align with our scaling framework to include:

- operational efficiencies
- market positioning
- financial wherewithal
- leadership effectiveness
- technological adoption
- organizational design
- and your overarching strategic alignment.

By delving into these areas (provided you're honest with your responses), the audit pinpoints both the areas of strength and potential constraints that could impede your growth trajectory. With incredible accuracy, it points out areas that are seldom recognized or readily apparent until they are surfaced—usually later in a business's lifecycle. And as an output result, the audit offers a detailed assessment that allows business leaders, like yourself, to celebrate the achievements that underscore your current success, but more importantly, to recognize areas that require attention and that are needed to be solved, or "unlocked," as we like to say, to prepare the company for "scale-readiness."

One of the audit's core benefits is its ability to highlight specific barriers to growth and distill these insights into a clear, actionable roadmap. It does this by applying a score—on the company as a whole (from 0 to 100) and for each of the six pillars of scaling—measuring both risk and resolvability. In the context the score assigned from our Scale Ready Audit, the scoring system considers two critical dimensions:

> **Risk**: This evaluates the potential negative impact on the business's scalability or enterprise value if the identified constraint remains ignored or unresolved. Higher risk indicates a greater threat to the business's growth potential and or value.

> **Resolvability**: This measures the difficulty level and the resource intensity required to address the constraint or capitalize on the opportunity. Lower resolvability scores suggest that the constraint is easier and less resource-heavy to resolve, while higher scores indicate more challenging and resource-intensive solutions.

This is where our work takes over to produce a more comprehensive strategic guide tailored to your business's unique circumstances, offering specific areas for us to focus on, ensuring each move we make is aligned with your broader vision for growth objectives.

[Note: While the Audit is our more comprehensive survey, performed with our engaged clients, you can access our abbreviated version, The "Scale Ready Self-Assessment" for your business and take the survey now to see your score, free of charge, at ReadyforScaling.com. Or, you can come back to it later on.]

Once we've clearly identified the company's constraints to scaling, using the Scale Ready Audit, we move on to the final element in our Golden Trio—assessing the entrepreneur's emotional fortitude.

Preparing for The Mental and Emotional Scale-Readiness Ride

From past experiences, we know the path to scaling is fraught with challenges, often emerging after the initial startup phase. However, while some challenges may inhibit our initial ability to scale, other challenges may remain hidden until further into the scaling phase, highlighting the importance of the Scale-Ready Self-Assessment.

This segues us into the realm of those unforeseen challenges and brings us to a pivotal aspect of scaling that goes beyond business models and market strategies and into a focus on you, the founder, and your mental and emotional readiness.

The structural readiness of a business to scale, while indispensable, is only one side of the coin. The other, equally critical, side pertains to the entrepreneur's personal preparedness to navigate this complex journey. The mental and emotional fortitude required to steer a business through the scaling process cannot be overstated. It involves cultivating a growth mindset, developing resilience against setbacks, and maintaining an emotional equilibrium amidst the turbulence of scaling.

As we delve into this section, let's explore the intrinsic qualities and characteristics that entrepreneurs and leaders must embody and employ to ensure not just the growth of their businesses but also the preservation of their well-being and vision. The reason this is vitally important? Because the journey ahead is as much about scaling the business as it is about scaling oneself. You'll need to prepare yourself for the inevitable ebbs and flows with stoicism and grace to steer the ship with a steady hand and a clear mind.

Cultivating a Growth Mindset

Scaling a business is not just about external growth. You'll find it's equally about personal development. Those entrepreneurs who succeed in scaling their companies are able to see challenges as opportunities to learn and improve. We've coined this term a "proportunity"—that is, turning problems into opportunities. This is a growth mindset, popularized by psychologist Carol Dweck, and is utterly essential as we embark on this journey, as it encourages resilience and a long-term view of setbacks and successes.

Building Emotional Readiness

The emotional fortitude, or mental readiness to scale, involves being prepared for the high demands that come with rapid growth. This includes managing stress, maintaining work-family harmony, and ensuring you don't lose sight of your personal well-being inside the hustle of scaling. Successful entrepreneurs are those who have prepared themselves to be *the calm* at the center of the storm, maintaining their focus and composure in the face of what will seem, at times, like insurmountable challenges.

The Core Leadership Qualities for Scaling

- **Passion for the Industry**

A genuine passion for your industry should be a driving force that keeps you motivated during the toughest as well as the best of times. This passion often translates into a deeper understanding of your customers' needs, the macro forces and trends shaping the industry, and a commitment to delivering value that goes beyond the superficial layers of business operations.

- **Grit and Determination**

Grit, defined by psychologist Angela Duckworth, is the passion and sustained persistence applied to long-term achievement, sometimes with no particular concern for rewards. For scaling entrepreneurs, this means having the perseverance and determination to see the scaling process through despite the hurdles. It's about playing the long game, believing in the short-term pain tradeoffs of committing to the dream of scaling your company.

- **Alignment with Personal and Company Values**

Harvard Business School's Clay Christensen's infamous last words each semester to his students were: "How can I be sure that I'll be happy in my career?" and "How can I be sure I'll stay out of jail?" As lighthearted as the second question is, it's worth considering. What Christensen was getting at in his second question is known as the "marginal cost" paradox.

That is, it's easier than you might think to make one unethical decision, just this one time or under this one unique circumstance, that leads down a slippery slope. It happens. Just look at Elizabeth Holmes (Theranos founder) and Sam Bankman-Fried (FTX founder) as recent examples where, once starting their ventures with honest intentions, at one point overlooked where the path of lies and deceit was ultimately headed, ignoring the full costs these choices entailed, and eventually landing themselves in prison.

As you are about to learn, the process of scaling your business is complex and multifaceted. Values, integrity, ethics, and maintaining alignment between your personal views and the business operations are critical for scaling your business without losing the essence of your soul. This alignment ensures that as your business grows, it reflects the values and ethical standards you hold dear, such as integrity, commitment to quality, respect for people, and doing what's right.

By layering in a solid foundation, uncovering the business's constraints, preparing yourself mentally and emotionally, and leading with the right blend of grit and vision, you can successfully guide your business through the nuances of rapid expansion.

If you're fired up and emotionally ready to take on the opportunistic challenge of scaling, then we'd like to take you through the very principles-centered framework that made our recent journey possible and has proven to work marvelously well for our clients...

Chapter 4

The Principles-Centered
Framework for Scaling

Sometimes, the most engaging tales begin in the most unassuming of ways.

Picture this: four eager partners with a fire in their bellies coming off their prior ventures, trying to figure out what business idea to focus on next. They decide to enter a business landscape they're utterly unfamiliar with, starting with an audacious dream and no outside capital or institutional debt. Fast forward four years. After allowing naivety to drive their curiosity for disrupting a stodgy industry, the four co-founders of QuickBox (a third-party logistics and order fulfillment company) transformed that dream into a whopping $100-million business, which they then sold to a progressive private equity firm. It sounds like the stuff of legends, but it's true. I was one of the founders who, as the CEO, led this company through its hyper-growth phases.

The secret? While we'd hesitate to call it that—is a reliable, battle-tested, and blazing-fast scaling framework. The framework we're about to share with you within these pages.

In the dynamic theater of business growth, the challenge of scaling your company is not just about achieving speed but mastering the art of expansion with precision and wisdom while keeping your wits intact. Throughout the seasoned journey of starting, building, and scaling four distinct enterprises of our own, coupled with the insights gleaned from working with hundreds of clients—CEOs, business founders, and entrepreneurs like you—we have crafted a robust, principles-centered framework for scaling that promises not just rapid growth but sustainable success. Our deep-rooted experience is further enriched by academic engagements, including teaching the theories behind these principles at the University of Denver, where I've been honored to be an adjunct professor to undergraduate and graduate students.

The framework we reveal here is composed of **five core principles**—time-tested yet continuously refined. Like the enduring values that underpin a great company, these principles have remained steadfast yet have evolved dramatically in their application over the years of being put into practice. This evolution has made them not only easier to implement but also more effective in driving meaningful impact within any aspiring, growing business.

This chapter is your gateway to understanding and leveraging this powerful blueprint, designed to help you scale your enterprise—to wherever your end goal lies—and without losing the essence of what made it unique in the first place.

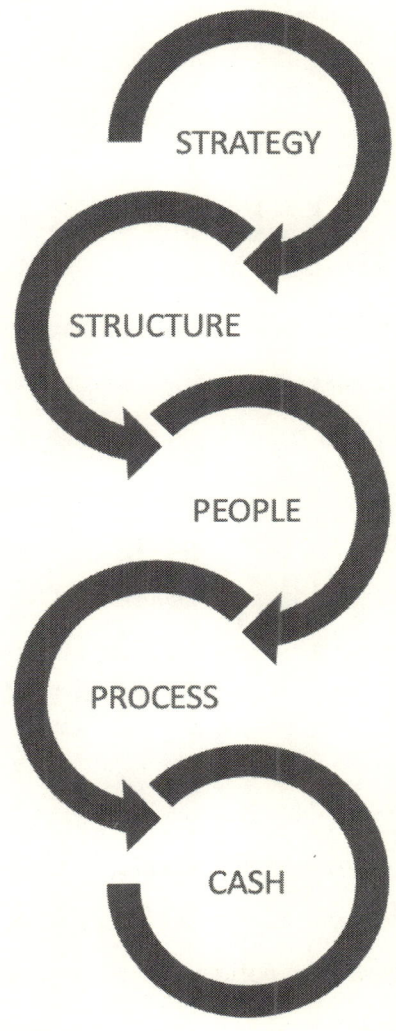

Mastering the Art of Scaling—A Proven Blueprint

In this chapter, we will holistically explore our scaling framework. Think of it as your game plan from here on out, which has been carefully designed for entrepreneurs eager to scale their ventures without losing their souls. We will briefly cover the five components of the scaling framework, and in the following chapters, we'll dive into each element much more comprehensively.

Strategy: Charting Your Path

At the heart of every successful scaling endeavor lies a clear and compelling strategy. This pillar examines the coherence and viability of your long-term plans, your competitive positioning, and how well your goals align with market opportunities. It's about ensuring your business's direction is not just aspirational but grounded in a clear understanding of your competitive landscape, internal capabilities, and customer needs. A well-defined strategy acts as your North Star, guiding every decision and action toward scalable growth. It lets everyone in the organization, from every position, align around a clear vision of "How we will compete and win." In essence, it serves as your rally cry.

Structure: Designing a Scalable Organization

As your business grows and becomes more complex, its foundation—the organization's structure—must keep pace and adapt. The

Structure pillar delves into the organizational design of your company, assessing whether it's built to withstand the pressures of scaling to ensure it's well aligned to deliver value by supporting your strategy. This includes evaluating your hierarchical arrangements, communication channels, and decision-making processes. A scalable structure is one that can adapt and evolve, allowing for the seamless integration of new teams, divisions, and technologies without losing efficiency or agility.

People: The Core of Your Growth

People are much more than just a line item on a financial spreadsheet; they are the lifeblood of your business. This pillar focuses on the talent within your organization, from leadership to the front lines. It's about ensuring you have the right people in the right roles, aligned with your company's culture, values, and vision.

As you scale, your team's ability to adapt, grow, and drive your vision forward becomes even more critical. This area assesses the readiness of your human resources to take on the challenges of scaling, spotlighting the need for continuous development, motivation, and alignment with your strategic goals.

Processes: Streamlining for Maximum Efficiency

Efficient processes, starting from a management operating system, are the backbone of any business—running smoothly without letting entropy build-up. In the context of scaling, the Processes pillar examines the efficiency, adaptability, and scalability of your operational workflows and systems. From ordering inventory, customer acquisition, to product delivery, every process must be optimized for efficiency and flexibility. (Within Process, we intend to share with you the "ultimate technology stack," after surveying hundreds of companies and vetting out the vast number of available options).

Streamlined processes not only enhance productivity and throughput but also ensure that, for the sake of speed, you're not sacrificing a consistent, high-quality experience for your customers as your business expands.

Cash: Fueling Your Expansion

Sustainable scaling requires sound financial management. The Cash pillar evaluates your financial health, focusing on cash flow, funding strategies, and resource allocation. It's about having the financial foresight and discipline to fuel your growth initiatives while maintaining a healthy balance sheet. This is because scaling often requires significant capital investments, and without a solid plan for managing finances, even the most promising businesses can flounder. (In addition, we intend to show you how to potentially self-fund growth with your company's internal operating capital.) This area scrutinizes your ability to manage financial challenges, invest in growth opportunities, and ensure the long-term financial sustainability of your scaling efforts.

Sequence Matters: The Choreography of Scaling

As we delve into your business, and if you've taken our Scale-Ready Self-Assessment, it may be tempting to tackle the most urgent or easiest issues first. However, adhering to the sequence of Strategy, Structure, People, Process, and Cash—*in that order*—is critical. This order ensures the foundational aspects support more complex initiatives that build on each other. Consider this sequence as the stages of building a skyscraper—from laying a solid foundation to raising the vertical beams and, finally, to painting and decoration. Skipping over steps, or excluding them altogether, can and certainly will compromise the integrity of your scaling efforts.

Now, let's circle back for a minute on this chapter's opening story—scaling QuickBox from scratch to $100 million. For us, the sequence of the five pillars of scaling was key. We began with a rock-solid strategy, built our structure to support it, gathered a team of world-class talent, streamlined our processes, and then, with internally generated cash flow as our priority to fund growth, we expanded at a pace that left our competitors in the dust. (We will delve much deeper into each of the keys to our scaling success in the upcoming chapters.)

By following our principles-centered framework and recognizing the importance of sequence, you can set the stage for sustainable growth—a testament to your leadership and dedication to your company's ethos.

Now, if you're ready to understand our approach to the implementation of each of the five pillars in the scaling framework, turn the page and let's jump right in…

PART TWO:

The Framework

Chapter 5

Strategy—Building a Winning Playbook

Have you ever stepped into a corporate office building where, amid the sleek decor of the waiting area or sprawling conference room, you notice a prominently displayed placard on the wall that proudly showcases the company's vision, values, and, occasionally, strategy? Likely crafted with an array of the latest buzzwords that string together into a verbose yet ultimately empty statement.

Often, the words chosen are the result of a consensus-driven process aimed at satisfying everyone's input. Unfortunately, the words fail to resonate meaningfully with either the company or its workforce. Worse yet, if you were to stroll through the office and question a handful of employees about their company's strategy, you'd likely be met with either blank stares, a tangled mess of explanations about the business operations, or a variety of differing responses.

The term "strategy" has become one of the most overused buzzwords in the business lexicon, yet it holds surprisingly little value to most employees within a company. This dilution typically stems from a profound misunderstanding of what strategy truly entails and its critical importance to every individual working within the organization.

Defining Strategy: What It Is *and Isn't*

The word "strategy" traces its roots back to the Greek word "strategos," which refers to a military general. This concept originally stemmed from the Latin phrase *Ars Bellica,* which translates to "the art of war."

In the context of business, just as in war, strategy involves careful planning and positioning of resources to achieve a specific objective despite existing opposition or competitive forces. It follows that a strategic path needs to be crafted to not only withstand potential threats but also leverage unique strengths to capture and maintain a competitive advantage.

At its core, strategy is about making informed choices to achieve long-term success. It is about deciding how you will compete, *and preferably win*, within your chosen market. It's not about tactics or operational activities; those are the functional steps we take to execute the strategy. Rather, strategy is the overarching plan or set of goals driving those activities.

In simplistic terms, a successful strategy serves as a rallying cry for your company—detailing a set of actions to gain and sustain a competitive advantage relative to the industry.

Scaling a business without a clear and compelling strategy is like captaining a ship in a thick fog without a map and compass. It's not just about moving forward; it's about moving in the *right* direction. This is where strategy steps into the spotlight.

I once had a mentor who imparted this crucial piece of wisdom: "Having a strategy that might be wrong is better than not having a strategy at all." It took me two decades of business leadership to fully grasp the essence of this profound statement and its pivotal role in a venture's success. It was only when I mastered the art of constructing effective strategies that I began to see substantial success in my own business endeavors.

Was strategy the sole factor? Not entirely, but it certainly brought unity and purpose to all our efforts. The reason is clear: *everything* we construct to make your company scale-ready hinges on the strategy. It either supports or services this framework, reiterating the importance of sequence in our scaling framework. The significance and value of a well-defined strategy, in other words, are immeasurable.

In business, a strategy that's complicated or vague might sound impressive in the boardroom, but it's often unhelpful on the frontline. Recall the tale of the emperor's new clothes, where not a single advisor dared to question the absurdity of the invisible garments, highlighting the peril of not challenging unclear assertions. Similarly, in the realm of business strategy, it is crucial to question and clarify every aspect to avoid marching proudly forward, only to realize you're not as covered as you thought. The magic within your company happens when a strategy is clear, compelling, actionable, *and* memorable. It becomes an important tool, a corporate-wide navigating guide, and a mantra for every team member to rally behind.

How To Craft a Winning Strategy

If we were operating within a Fortune 100 corporation, we would likely dedicate hundreds of hours to preparation, analysis, and assessment, often convening large committees and retreating offsite for days to meticulously craft a strategy. Such strategies are designed to secure superior performance and sustainable competitive advantages over rivals. However, that scenario doesn't exactly align with our reality, does it.

We are entrepreneurs and founders—dynamic, busy individuals who are deeply involved in the day-to-day operations of our ventures. Unlike large corporations, we often lack a large executive team or a plethora of analysts at our disposal. That being said, these limitations don't diminish the importance of thorough preparation and taking a mindful approach toward crafting a solid strategy. In fact, they highlight it. Gathering your C-suite team or even just your co-founding partner for an offsite session is a vitally important step in the process. It allows for focused, undistracted development of a purposeful strategy.

Given our limited resources, it's essential that we create a strategy that is not only practical but one that garners full alignment and belief from your team. Such a strategy will not only inspire your team to rally behind it but will guide nearly every decision as we advance. In essence, we need to build a streamlined yet compelling strategy that is both memorable and resonates deeply to propel our business toward its enterprise goals.

Here's how we do it…

To develop a robust strategy, we start by answering five pivotal questions about your business's aspiration, direction, and purpose. These five questions are fundamental to any strategy development process.

Phase I: Build a North Star by Answering The 5 Business Strategy Questions

1. *What are our aspirations as a company?*

Another way to consider this question: what do we want to be when we grow (or scale) up, and answering the perplexing yet most important question, *why* do we exist? (In other words, what reason do we have to exist; what is our greater mission beyond financial metrics?)

2. *Where are we going to compete?*

This is about making the choice, in terms of market segmentation, where you believe your products or services will have the strongest competitive advantage. In other words, what industry vertical do you intend to compete in; and where, geographically, will you participate (such as local, regional, national, international, etc.)? And *who* is the ideal customer of your product or service?

3. *How will we win against our key competitors?*

This is the heart of strategy. It's about carving out a unique space in the market and determining how you'll differentiate yourself and protect your competitive advantage. For this question, we recommend using our proprietary Diamond Strategic Positioning Grid, which is found on ReadyforScaling.com. Deliberately choosing where you won't compete is just as vital and impactful as determining where you will play to win.

4. *What capabilities are needed to achieve success?*

Here, think about the skills, resources, and assets critical for delivering your value proposition and standing apart from competitors. This is where you'll take inventory of your existing capabilities, core competencies, and assets and look for any gaps.

5. *How will we measure our success?*

To effectively answer this, we'll need to focus on setting clear (even if just directionally), quantifiable targets such as growth in market share, revenue expansion, or key marketing metrics like customer retention. Additionally, you should assess qualitative factors and leading indicators like brand strength (which can be evaluated through Net Promoter Score) and customer satisfaction, such as online reviews, to ensure a comprehensive understanding of your progress toward achieving the strategic vision.

Finally, it's important to answer one more vitally important, fundamental question:

What problem are we solving?

This question revolves around identifying the problem your product or service solves, how it does so, and understanding what makes your business unique and why customers should choose you over competitors.

Interestingly, I've noticed that many business owners struggle to answer this fundamental question succinctly and confidently. If you can't pinpoint the *exact* problem your business addresses, you're missing the mark from the onset. This question should be at the forefront of your considerations in developing your strategy because, as one would discover in our "Formula for Scalability," there's a direct correlation between the size and complexity of the problem you're solving and the potential rewards of success in your business venture.

The larger and more intricate the problem, the greater the potential for scalability and overall success of your organization. Understanding this relationship is important as it highlights the importance of deeply comprehending the challenging issue your company aims to address. By fully grasping the nature of the problem and deeply understanding *why* your company exists, you can maximize the growth and profitability of your enterprise.

Access The Strategic Roadmap to help you craft your own clear, compelling, and memorable strategic plan at ReadyForScaling.com/Resources

Next, we dive into consolidating our findings to formulate a power-fully clear, compelling, and memorable strategic mantra. Here's how we do this...

Phase II: Crafting Simplicity into Our Strategy (It Matters)

Over the years, as I've built and led companies, I experimented with crafting complex and verbose strategic statements. Despite my efforts to communicate these strategies effectively, they never truly resonated with our employees. The problem wasn't that these messages were ignored. Rather, they were simply too convoluted to grasp, too lengthy to recall, and lacked the compelling force necessary to excite and convince our team that these strategies were our ticket to success.

Through these experiences, I've learned that a clear and concise strategy consistently proves to be the most impactful. Instead of overcomplicating things, I discovered that by addressing our five critical strategy questions (those we answered earlier in this chapter) and gaining a deep understanding of the market and our competitors, we could distill our strategy down into a single sentence or phrase. This approach not only made our strategic direction easier to communicate but also more memorable and engaging for our team, enhancing our overall effectiveness and alignment.

Allow me to share how this exercise is put into practice...

To effectively distill a complex strategy into a simple yet powerful sentence or phrase, we would begin by gathering your executive team together for a strategic session. Armed with a comprehensive market and competitor analysis as well as an internal business assessment, we'd then use the five critical questions to probe the essence of your strategy (focused on the Diamond Strategic Positioning Grid). Then, we'd identify your aspirations, the market you'll compete in, your ideal customers, unique offerings, core strengths, and success metrics.

During this session, we'll encourage a brainstorming process to generate a variety of strategic statements that encapsulate the insights from these questions against the backdrop of a single question: "How do we believe we can compete, *and win*, in our chosen market?"

It's vital to narrow these down through hearty discussion, focusing on clarity, impact, and alignment with your internal strengths and business goals. If you have the time, and fortitude, you could also test the resonance and clarity of the top choices with a broader group of stakeholders to ensure the statement is both inspiring and credible.

Select the phrase that best resonates, refine it to enhance its power and conciseness, and then—and this is vitally important—implement it across all company communications and touchpoints with employees. Don't be afraid to overcommunicate it. In fact, *strive to overcommunicate* throughout the entire organization. This final strategic phrase, if crafted well, should serve as a rallying cry that not only aligns but also motivates your entire organization, embedding the strategic vision into the company's culture, operations, and daily decision-making.

Here's an example of how we guided one of our clients to construct their winning strategic mantra...

A Mini-Case in Strategic Alignment

In the dynamic and competitive world of CBD-based consumer products, one of our client companies sought to redefine its strategic direction through a meticulously planned offsite in Los Angeles.

To set the tone, we orchestrated a two-day strategic session atop a scenic rooftop conference venue along Sunset Boulevard. We invited key personnel from the director level and above who were associated with each brand. The company's CEO was humble enough to adopt a participatory role, ensuring an unguided flow of ideas rather than steering discussions, which was needed for genuine engagement and team participation.

We pre-assigned tasks to specific groups to enhance focus and productivity. One team delved into analyzing external environmental, societal, and economic factors along with macro trends affecting the CBD industry. Another evaluated the company's internal strengths, core competencies, and capabilities, as well as any notable gaps. This preparatory work was vital for grounding the strategy sessions in both current market realities and the company's operational capabilities.

The offsite commenced with a reaffirmation of the company's vision and values, leading to a significant moment of alignment when the value of "innovation" was debated and eventually replaced. This change reflected a shift toward emphasizing the team's strong work ethic, and as such, agreed the phrase "High Collaboration" resonated more authentically with the team's true operational ethos, fostering a robust debate that underscored the team's commitment to these core principles.

During the intensive sessions that followed, the teams presented their findings, engaging in vigorous discussions that were visualized through whiteboarding on oversized notepads. This collaborative analysis highlighted three important areas: (i) the company's swift responsiveness to emerging product trends; (ii) its adeptness at securing organic traffic and dominating Google's top search results; and (iii) a profound commitment to customer care post-purchase. These core competencies were then juxtaposed with existing capabilities to identify overlap and any strategic gaps.

A salient aspect of our framework involved using the Diamond Strategic Positioning Grid, which helped position each brand according to the differentiation of its products based on distinct features and its market protection from competitors. This exercise provided clarity on competitive positioning, reinforcing the company's ability to quickly develop and market new products, and leverage its unique online marketing model that could preemptively capture market share before competitors could react, thereby allowing the company to reap the lion's share of captured revenues.

The culmination of these discussions and analyses was the crafting of a powerful business strategy mantra: *"Win the product category; build lasting brand affinity."* This mantra encapsulated a clear, compelling strategic mantra that was easy to communicate, simple to recollect, and rallied the team around a unified vision.

Equally important, it was strategically aligned with the company's strengths and capabilities, providing an easy, go-to guide for future decision-making, resource allocation, and annual initiatives. In other words, it steered the company to stay focused on efforts to win prominent category listings within search engines on new products and ensure customer obsession in all post-purchase activities. If anyone's actions veered from serving this strategic directive, it would undoubtedly be questioned.

This summarized case study exemplifies how a strategic offsite, using a framework like ours, can catalyze profound alignment within a company, enabling it to articulate a coherent and actionable business strategy that leverages its intrinsic strengths to achieve competitive dominance and sustainable growth.

Consider the following examples of strategic mantras from some leading companies—showing how even the largest and most successful organizations follow this practice. Try to appreciate the genius of simplicity within these real-world examples:

Southwest Airlines. Southwest didn't overcomplicate things. Their strategic mantra, "*Wheels Up!*," encapsulated their focus on quick turnarounds and efficiency—through singular routes (not a hub-and-spoke like other airlines), seat yourself boarding, and relying on only one type of airplane across their fleet. It wasn't about plush seating or gourmet meals; it was about getting those wheels off the ground and ensuring timely departures and arrivals.

Chick-fil-A, "*Where Good Meets Gracious*": At its core, this isn't just about serving quality chicken. Notice they didn't say anything about great food. Rather, it's a promise of a delightful experience where customers are treated with kindness and respect. And if you've ever been greeted with a "My pleasure" at one of their outlets and felt generally good or cheerful after leaving, you know how they deliver on that promise.

Home Depot, "*The One Home Depot*" (emphasis on The One): This isn't just a statement of unity; it's a commitment to consistent quality and service across all their locations, under one location within their outlet stores. Whether you walk into a Home Depot in

Atlanta, Austin, or Los Angeles, the expectation is a uniform experience, and they strive to make it a good one by having everything you could want for your DIY home projects under one roof.

Crafting Your Winning Strategy

Strategy is more than just an academic buzzword. It's where *everything* starts from, and serves into, within any ambitious business venture. It's the bridge between where a company currently stands and where it aspires to be. And it should serve as a North Star and rallying cry for the entire company. As we endeavor to scale-ready your business, let's keep these strategy fundamentals in mind to ensure not just growth but growth that's sustainable and aligned with your core values and vision.

Access The Strategic Roadmap to help you craft your own clear, compelling, and memorable strategic plan at ReadyForScaling.com/resources

As the renowned military strategist and philosopher Sun Tzu once said, "Strategy without tactics is the slowest route to victory. Tactics without strategy is the noise before defeat." So, let's continue our journey by jumping into the next pillar of scaling—Structure—and learn how to design an organization to impeccably support your newly defined strategy…

Full Case Study: QuickBox—The Strategy of Irresistible Engagement

In an industry where traditional business models reigned supreme and hadn't changed for nearly a century, QuickBox, a third-party logistics and order fulfillment center (aka 3PL), emerged as a disruptor.

The origin of QuickBox traces back to a serendipitous meeting of four entrepreneurs, including me, each at a crossroads after wrapping up previous ventures. Our paths converged over dinner in Broomfield, Colorado, one October evening, followed by several more brainstorming sessions. We were on a quest for our next big project. The burgeoning direct-to-consumer, e-commerce, and consumer goods landscape presented a golden opportunity. Despite our collective lack of experience in logistics, warehousing, or fulfillment, our fresh perspectives were exactly what was needed to innovate. In essence, we had a strong inclination that it was an industry ripe for disruptive innovation.

By January, we had signed a lease for a sprawling 105,000-square-foot warehouse in Denver, Colorado. From the outset, we adhered to our meticulously crafted framework that emphasized the importance of starting with a clear, compelling strategy to steer the company. This strategy would not only align our team with our goals but also carve out a competitive advantage in a fiercely competitive market. As founders, we retreated for a two-day intensive offsite, where debates and discussions flowed until we reached a collective "buy-in" on what would become our game-changing, winning strategy:

"Easy in; Impossible to get out!"

Far from divisive, it was not about creating a trap. Rather, this mantra was about delivering such exceptional value, through added offerings (above typical 3PLs), that we would become vitally integral to our clients' operations, making the thought of leaving us unfathomable.

The Genesis of the Strategy

During the strategic planning process, the QuickBox founders recognized an opportunity to invigorate a stagnant industry plagued by uninspired services provided at a basic commodity level by nearly every competing 3PL. The founders agreed that the industry was ripe for disruption and identified two pivotal areas to transform service delivery.

First, we aimed to streamline the sales and onboarding process for new clients to engage with our services, ensuring that entry into the ecosystem was as seamless and swift as possible. The real competitive advantage, however, would stem from the second focus: layering in an array of additional products and valuable services complemented by an out-standing customer experience. This strategy was designed so that choosing to leave QuickBox would mean a significant forfeiture of value for our clients. Essentially, QuickBox set out to become not just a 3PL provider but an indispensable partner in our clients' operations.

Here's how QuickBox developed and leveraged its "easy in, impossible to get out" strategy:

As the founders of QuickBox, we delved into the strategic positioning of the new venture and used our proprietary Diamond Strategic Positioning Grid—a tool that helps clarify the competitive angle and understand the necessary tradeoffs in a new business venture's market-entry strategy.

Initially, we chose to focus on cost leadership to secure a foothold in the 3PL industry, a sector notorious for its high barriers to entry. By leveraging competitive pricing, and in parallel, fostering deep relationships with clients, QuickBox aimed to distinguish itself from the competition.

However, differentiation was equally key to our strategy. From the outset, QuickBox decided to avoid competing through technological innovations, such as robotics or robust user-interfaced systems, a purposeful tradeoff we planned to explore later in the business's lifecycle when more resources and experience were accumulated. Instead, our immediate focus was on being distinct through added-value offerings.

These value offerings included selling product inventory directly to clients, providing custom packaging solutions, offering competitive shipping rates, and managing specialized services such as white-glove returns and Amazon store management. These services were not only practical but designed to embed QuickBox deeply into the operations of our clients, making the service hard to replace.

Looking toward the future, as founders, we were well aware that as QuickBox matured, the initial strategy of cost leadership would need to evolve. The plan was to gradually shift toward a focus on enhanced service, operational excellence, and cutting-edge technology. This transition aimed to further differentiate QuickBox in the market, introducing innovative technological advancements that would improve operational efficiency, accuracy, and transparency.

Such advancements would not only solidify QuickBox's market position but also enable it to offer premium services at higher price points, thereby navigating the company from cost leadership to a value-based, technology-driven entity.

As a result, QuickBox didn't just acquire customers; it built a loyal community of clients. The churn rate was among the lowest in the industry, and customer satisfaction ratings soared. This strategy propelled QuickBox into a leadership position, outpacing competitors that were still trying to play the old game.

In retrospect, the "Easy in; Impossible to get out" strategy was like hosting a party that's so good that guests don't want to leave. Sure, the company faced challenges—from logistical nightmares to the occasional misstep in customer expectations. Still, our obsessive focus on delivering unmatched value made QuickBox a name synonymous with innovation and customer loyalty. And, best of all, it produced multiples of higher-than-average profit margins.

Access The Strategic Roadmap to help you craft your own clear, compelling, and memorable strategic plan at ReadyForScaling.com/resources

Chapter 6

Structure—Architecting an Organization for Scale

The true essence of organizational structure, in its simplest form, is aligning the company to execute its strategy to achieve market dominance. Structure, if designed correctly, acts as the backbone of a company, supporting and shaping its growth trajectory. Above all, effective organizational design is critical to scaling because it directly impacts a company's ability to respond to market demands, innovate, and maintain superior operational velocity.

When structure is aligned with strategy, companies can expect to experience enhanced coordination and communication across departments. This coordination leads to quicker decision-making and improved overall performance. As you scale, the complexity of operations typically increases, making a well-designed structure even more important. Without it, we've seen companies continue to struggle with inefficiencies, redundancies, and internal conflicts that hinder growth. This is called entropy. And if left unaddressed, it can literally bring a fast-moving company to a grinding halt.

Moreover, the frequency of structural assessment and redesign should align with each major growth phase. Often, this means revisiting the structure about every six months, sometimes sooner, and certainly not longer than a year. This cadence is especially paramount in fast-growing, scaling companies.

Understanding Structure in Business Growth

Structure is perhaps the most pivotal yet frequently misunderstood element in scaling a business, particularly when trying to surge beyond the first $1 million milestone or attempting to make another $10-million, or even $25-million, leap.

In my previous venture, QuickBox, where even as we produced larger financial metrics, we achieved over 100 percent year-on-year growth during our scaling phase, I discovered that redesigning our organizational structure approximately every six months or so was critical. This continuous restructuring, I am confident, was essential to our breakthrough past the $100-million mark in under five years.

Ignoring the need for a dynamic organizational structure, on the other hand, can be a substantial barrier to growth. Companies that fail to adapt their structure to fit their evolving external environment risk falling into organizational inertia—much like purgatory—where an outdated structure stifles growth and innovation and can even erode company culture.

And this is where, far too often, we see companies fall into the trap of conflating an organizational chart with company structure. I certainly made this mistake during my earlier ventures. That is, if we don't yet understand the root cause of why the company is stalling out, we often start with an organizational chart to find where the business is getting it wrong. This backward approach involves populating a hierarchical chart with titles and roles and then rushing to fill open slots with available candidates rather than designing roles around strategic needs and business functions based on a sound structure.

Structure as a Catalyst for Growth

Before we dive into Structure, let us first review the foundational principles of organizational design, which are based on three criteria, that will help us clarify how to achieve alignment between our strategy and structure. They are:

- Function
- Location
- Authority

Remember this—FLA: it will come in handy throughout this chapter.

After working with both large and small companies, we have identified key milestones in which an organization should undergo a structural redesign, based on these criteria:

> **Phase I—the early-stage solopreneur**, usually after breaking the $1-million revenue threshold

> **Phase II—building out a leadership team**, normally once the company surpasses $10 million in revenue.

> And finally, **Phase III—when a company is butting up against a revenue ceiling**, typically sub-$50 million revenue that they can't seem to break through.

Let's break down each of these phases within the context of their organizational design…

Phase One: Transitioning from Solopreneur to Strategic Hiring

When launching a new business venture, it's common for founders, especially in the initial stages—be it the first year or until hitting the first $1 million in revenue—to take on a multitude of roles. Essentially, you become the company's operations, handling everything from marketing to HR management to sales to customer service.

This period is invaluable as it immerses you deeply in every aspect of your business, giving you a holistic understanding of its operations.

However, this approach, while necessary at first, can quickly become a limitation and barrier to growth. Once the business achieves a certain level of revenue, and once there are sufficient resources—either through revenue generation or an investment infusion—it becomes possible, and necessary, to bring in additional capabilities. This expansion is critical because, without it, further scaling becomes unmanageable.

A common pitfall for many early-stage entrepreneurs occurs when they ask, "Who should be my first hire?" However, this question, often asked during a critical moment of a business's growth, is not the most important one when considering how to design your organizational structure.

Instead, the pivotal question we encourage you to ask is, "*What complementary strengths, based on the needed capabilities to execute our strategy, do I need to scale to the next level of revenue?*"

This inquiry shifts the focus from filling a predetermined position, or seeking an ideal candidate, to identifying the responsibilities to be delegated, or shifted rather, that will most effectively assist you in delivering on your strategic vision.

This is a lesson I learned the hard way in my early entrepreneurial endeavors. Initially, I was overly concerned with populating an executive org chart, thinking I needed a CFO, COO, CTO, then a CMO, and so on, without critically assessing which functions would truly benefit our strategic execution and deliver the intended value to our customers. This approach (conflating an org chart with structure), focused more on titles than on strategic function, was far from effective and led to several early missteps.

To navigate this crucial stage of growth, it's essential to align your hiring process with your organizational strategic needs rather than filling up a traditional org chart with titles. By focusing on the skills and capabilities that genuinely complement your own and address your business's operational demands, you position your venture for the next level of scaling with your first key hire.

Phase Two: Building a Cohesive Leadership Team

As the business progresses and revenue approaches crossing the $10-million mark, building a talented, functional-based leadership team based on a unified strategic vision becomes the next critical step when designing the appropriate organizational structure. This stage focuses on diversifying roles tailored to individual strengths and business needs, establishing governance structures, and ensuring the team is dynamic enough to adapt to market demands while maintaining the company's core values.

In the early stages of business growth, though, it is imperative to consolidate the organizational structure and center it around the core processes and embedded competencies of the company. We cannot overstate this enough. That is, the key driving functions of the business should dictate your organizational design needs. Let's explore this through the lens of a practical example...

A Mini-Case in Organizational Design of a Rapidly Growing Apparel Company

Consider a rapidly growing apparel company we consulted. They specialize in designing and selling innovative, comfortable, and stylish athleisure wear. Founded by two sisters, one's husband, and a long-time friend, the company had quickly outgrown its initial early-adoption customer base and was rapidly expanding its reach.

As is common in the nascent stages of a business, the small team of founders found themselves overwhelmed, juggling more tasks than they could manage, and straying from their areas of expertise. Recognizing the need for a strategic reorganization, we embarked on a simple yet effective exercise to realign their organizational structure to better support their growth. The key to this exercise, most importantly, is about the what (function), where (location), and the power (authority)—and *then* who.

The first step was to clearly define the primary functions vital to generating enterprise value. After a thorough review, we identified four key functional areas: product design, inventory planning, customer activation, and brand management.

Next, and this is the difficult part, approaching the organizational redesign with a clean slate—free from the constraints of existing titles and preconceived roles—which allowed us to strategically position each function within the organization for optimal effectiveness. During this phase, we focused on clearly defining the leadership roles for each of the four functional areas, ensuring that responsibilities, accountability, and authority were explicitly established for each leadership position.

Finally, we determined the best personnel fits for these leadership roles based on expertise, interest, and proven competence rather than seniority or previous titles. Keep in mind, there are not any titles granted until we get to this stage and assign appropriate titles. Titles, especially for legacy roles, should not dictate their location. Rather, location should dictate the most suitable title to match the primary function served by the role.

This approach allowed us to draft an initial skeletal organization chart based on the newly proposed structure, which we then refined by assigning team members, including the founders, to support roles under each function, ensuring comprehensive coverage of all critical areas.

This methodical realignment revealed a glaring gap inside of inventory planning and brand management. The identification of these gaps enabled us to strategically recruit new talent to fill these crucial roles, thus completing the leadership team. This restructuring had a transformative impact on the company, enhancing its execution capabilities and aligning its structure with the strategic goals.

The result was a dramatic increase in efficiency and growth, propelling them past the $25-million revenue mark and setting the stage for a subsequent surge to $50-million.

This case study example underscores the importance of a thoughtfully designed organizational structure in scaling businesses. By focusing on core functions and aligning roles and responsibilities around them, your company can enhance the strategic execution and set a solid foundation for sustained growth.

Phase Three: Overhaul Restructuring for Market Resurgence

The third phase of organizational development is often the most complex and challenging to overcome. It emerges when a company stabilizes within a certain revenue bracket, struggling to advance beyond the current revenue ceiling.

This plateau typically necessitates a thorough evaluation focused on two key areas: (i) the alignment of the organizational structure with the current business lifecycle and the evolving profile of the customers it serves; and (ii) a comprehensive assessment of the executive team's capabilities, ambition, and experience in fostering growth be-yond the current phase.

This stage may involve transitioning from a smaller leadership team to a more robust and diverse group of leaders who can bring fresh perspectives, market or industry experience in a growth company, and very specific skills to the table. Alternatively, if a robust leadership team is already in place, this phase might require an honest and criti-cal reassessment and possible realignment of the structure or roles. We find this is quite common, especially among companies that have stalled growth.

Our experience with fast-growing companies has shown us that the strategies and leadership that contributed to past successes are not necessarily the same ones that will propel a company to new heights. Often, executives who were effective in earlier stages find them-selves stretched too thin or lacking the necessary skills to lead the company as it grows. They may be over-titled, promoted beyond their level of competence, or simply not the right cultural fit for the organization's evolving dynamics. Here's an actual example of how this typically unfolds...

A Mini-Case in Breaking Through the Glass Revenue Ceiling

One of the more complex businesses I founded and ran, a nutritional supplement company, had hit the proverbial growth ceiling, sitting

around $60 million market capitalization. We enjoyed a well-estab-
lished executive leadership team with loads of industry experience,
yet through (what would later evolve into our) more comprehensive
"Scale-Ready Self-Assessment," we were able to reveal an alarming
misalignment.

Our internal assessment had unearthed that the company's organizational structure was no longer suited to the complexity introduced
by its brand expansion strategy. We had bolted on and developed
new brands—a sports nutrition, weight loss, energy, children's and
natural vitamin brand lines, ultimately managing five unique consumer goods brands, with vastly different customer bases, within
our portfolio. While there were some operational overlaps among
the brands, distinct differences in brand strategies were causing confusion and inefficiency across the organization.

The most vocal brand often captured the most resources, leading to
skewed priorities and compromised throughput. Internal politics
further exacerbated these issues, undermining efficiency and eroding our company's culture.

We conducted a detailed review of our strategic execution history,
along with a thorough assessment of each brand's capabilities and
core competencies. This examination helped us better understand
how functions across the brands interacted and where operational
overlaps and distinctions lay. It became clear that our existing hier-

archical organizational structure was inadequate to support the diverse and complex nature of the multi-brand company we had evolved into.

To address these challenges and inefficiencies, we opted to transition to a "hybrid-matrix" organizational structure that incorporated elements of shared services alongside dedicated brand management teams. This structure was popular among the larger consumer packaged goods companies, and so we theorized it would work just as well for us, given our brand segregation. The idea, we thought, was to present a new structure designed to optimize both efficiency and brand autonomy.

Key operational functions, such as accounting, legal, and human resources, were centralized into shared services across all brands. And each brand was assigned its own teams, and a brand authoritarian (like a CEO for the brand) to execute on their primary functions of product development, creative and marketing, and customer service.

This realignment allowed each of our five brand teams to focus on innovating and executing strategies that were tailored to *their* specific market needs without the encumbrance of competing for internal resources. In the end, this new organizational design provided the foundational support we needed across all brands, reducing prioritization friction, and streamlining operations, thereby unlocking our potential to spur growth once again.

As you can see, this example exemplifies the critical need for adaptive organizational design in companies managing multiple brands or product lines or when entering new revenue ranges, business life cycles, or within the constraints of complex operations. A well-conceived structure that aligns with the complexities of the business is imperative for clear strategic execution and sustainable growth. Addressing these challenges head-on is vital to break through to the next level of organizational development.

Now, let's jump into how you can design the ideal organizational structure for your business…

Designing Your Organization for Strategic Growth

Appreciate that designing your organization strategically is essential for scaling effectively. It's about positioning your company to not only meet current demands but to anticipate and adapt to future challenges.

Here's the step-by-step guide we use with our clients to design the appropriate structure—setting up the organization for success and keeping in mind that the focus should be on aligning organizational roles with strategic goals rather than merely filling positions.

Step 1: Map Key Functions or Processes

Begin by identifying the core functions or processes that drive your company—ideally, those that generate revenue or serve to grow the customer base. These are the activities critical to your business's success, from product development to sales to customer service. Understanding these key functions will provide a basis for the framework to structure your organization.

Step 2: Analyze the Value Chain

For each key function, map out the entire value chain. This includes detailing each of the major steps of the process from inception to completion and, importantly, showing its relationship to cash flow. Understanding how each function contributes to the financial health of the company is crucial for prioritizing resource allocation.

Step 3: Assign Leadership Roles

Appoint a leadership role for each major function (which could be you, for the time being). Choosing the appropriate role for each key function should consider the needed expertise, leadership ability, and how their capabilities align with the company's strategic goals. These leadership roles will be pivotal in driving the success of their respective functions.

A common pitfall in organizational design is to assign individuals (or names of persons) to roles too early in the process. This approach often leads to misalignment, as decisions are influenced more by personnel than by strategic needs. Instead, focus first on defining the roles and responsibilities based on strategic objectives and functional roles before slotting people into positions with titles. Remember, with our approach, you should address the *what* first, then the *who*.

Step 4: Define Reporting, Authority, and Communication Lines

Once leadership roles are in place, draw clear reporting and communication lines to other supporting roles within the function. This structure should facilitate efficient information flow and decision-making processes within the organization, ensuring all teams are aligned and cohesive. At all costs, avoid drawing dotted lines between two roles where another solid line already exists, or having a role report into two different leaders—either of these, in our experience, usually doesn't work out well to support a cohesive structure.

Step 5: Title Assignment

After the roles are defined, authority is assigned, and the right leaders are matched with their respective functions, you can then assign official titles. This step should come last to avoid the distractions and politics often associated with title assignments. Titles should reflect the roles and responsibilities, not the other way around. This final step might feel like you're "shuffling the deck," but that's quite alright, and as a result, new or changed titles may emerge from this exercise.

Structure as a Strategic Asset

In sum, constructing and implementing the right organizational structure is more than just filling out an org chart. It's about creating a dynamic system that supports strategic goals to facilitate efficient communication and effective execution. When done correctly, a well-thought-out organizational structure not only reduces friction within the company but also significantly enhances how quickly and effectively work gets done in terms of operational velocity.

As your business grows and reaches new stages, continually optimizing and realigning this structure is key to unlocking further growth and achieving sustained scaling success. Our approach ensures that every aspect of your organization contributes to its overarching strategic goals, making your structure a true asset in the competitive landscape.

Alright. If you're ready to dive into the next pillar, *People*, then turn the page and let's get started...

Mini Case Study: How Mastering the Matrix Allowed a Holding Company to Successfully Manage a Multitude of Brands

Introduction: A Symphony of Brands

A client of ours, a diverse enterprise managing several brands in the booming human and pet CBD supplement market, was confronted by the classic challenge of scaling amidst a wildly competing set of brand priorities within a robust and ambitious organization. As a result, they hit a growth ceiling at around $35 million and had been stuck there for nearly 18 months, unable to break through. They boasted a robust executive leadership team, yet through our hands-on "Scale-Ready Audit," we revealed a significant misalignment.

Originally adopting a traditional flat-hierarchical built organizational structure, the company struggled with inefficiencies and miscommunications that stifled growth.

Our comprehensive Scale Ready Assessment illuminated these issues vividly, revealing the conventional setup as ill-suited for its multifaceted operations and rapid growth. This misalignment was not just a barrier to efficiency but also a fundamental constraint on the company's potential to continue to scale all their brands effectively.

Enter an Organizational Redesign

Introducing the Hybrid-Matrix: Our solution was the innovative hybrid-matrix model, which integrates the clarity of a traditional hierarchy with the flexibility of a matrix structure. This model supports efficient resource allocation and management across various functions while allowing each brand to maintain individual operational teams focused on specific market dynamics and customer needs. It's a model similarly deployed by multi-brand companies like Procter & Gamble, Unilever, and Church & Dwight, among other consumer packaged goods companies.

Implementation: Implementing this model involved a structured 30-day transition period. We established autonomous brand-specific teams alongside shared service departments to ensure tailored strategies and operations per brand.

These shared services—including HR, legal, technology, compliance, and finance—serve as the supportive backbone, providing consistent services across all brands.

Challenges and Triumphs: The initial rollout of the hybrid-matrix model was met with inevitable adjustments and some obstinacy. The reorganization required employees to adapt to new roles and interdepartmental dynamics quickly.

Although the transition period was marked by some confusion and the need to recalibrate some roles and responsibilities, the strategic realignment immediately led to enhanced communication and operational clarity.

Training and Communication: To ease the transition, we facilitated targeted training programs to acquaint staff with their new roles and the nuances of the hybrid model. Regular communication forums and a structured format and cadence for team or functional meetings were also established, becoming essential in smoothing over initial teething problems and fostering a culture of openness, teamwork, and adaptability.

The Bigger Picture: Scaling with Precision

The adoption of the hybrid-matrix model transformed our clients' operational velocity and clarity around brand priorities. Post-implementation, each of the six brands began to operate with a newfound focus and efficiency. Dedicated teams enabled quicker responses to market changes and more innovative product development. Simultaneously, the shared resources ensured that all brands benefited from high-level expertise and support without duplicating overheads. This strategic overhaul not only improved day-to-day operations and related throughput but also significantly boosted overall market responsiveness and profitability.

This transformation encapsulates a critical lesson we learned early on for rapidly growing companies: effective scaling is contingent on the ability to adapt internal structures strategically. Proper alignment of organizational structure with the business's strategy and market demands is paramount, ensuring that every segment of the company contributes optimally toward those collective strategic goals and phases of the business or brand's life cycle.

Chapter 7

People—The Heartbeat of Scalable Success

Behind every successful company lies its people—passionate, determined, and ever-evolving. Make no mistake about it: the strength of any leader lies in the quality of their team. As you set your business on the fast track of scaling, remember that your level of success will be directly tied to the level of your talent and their evolution with your company. In the world of exponential growth, your team's consistent performance, adaptability, leadership, and culture play a pivotal role in your company's ability to scale.

In the thrilling journey of scaling a business, the people you bring on board shouldn't be viewed as participants merely to help you get things done, or an expense line item on a spreadsheet. Rather, they become the embedded drivers of your company's next level of growth. And, attracting the *right* people can make or break the process.

The Phases of Building a Scale-Ready Team

Phase One: This journey of talent attraction normally begins right around the time your company surpasses $1 million in annual revenue (in Phase I, referencing back to Structure in the previous chapter). Navigating beyond the "founder's trap"—a fundamental yet critical phase where stepping aside as the founder-operator—to empower others becomes essential for growth.

The initial hire—your first true test—is your most critical. This first key leadership role you hire should *complement* your abilities and directly support the core drivers of your company's growth. This is not just about filling a vacant seat but strategically aligning talent with who is best suited to get your business a giant step closer to your vision.

I cannot emphasize this enough: finding exceptional talent that excels in an area where you don't and clearly aligns with a primary function of the company's core driver of growth is essential to get right on the first attempt. The wrong first hire, on the other hand, can set you back months, sometimes longer, trying to recover.

Phase Two: Following this stage, and once you've surpassed about $10 million in annual revenues (during Phase II), entrepreneurs will encounter what I like to call the "growth leap." This is a pivotal moment when the focus must shift from a couple of key players driving the business to constructing a true leadership team. Thinking back to our first hire, these new team members should be meticulously drafted in the same way, around the key functions that propel the business forward—based on the Structure we defined in the previous chapter.

At this stage, it's easiest to think of the business in terms of "front-end" and "back-end" functions. The front end encompasses all customer-facing activities up to the point of purchase, requiring personnel who excel in engagement, activation, and sales. The back end, on the other hand, deals with everything post-purchase, which includes managing the customer experience and ensuring the service or product delivery is seamless and meeting, or better yet, exceeding standards.

This dichotomy ensures both sides of the customer journey are optimized for success and scalability. However, in the early part of the scaling phase, I normally lean more toward "stacking the deck" in favor of the front end—those functions that are driving the growth of the company. Then, as the company meets certain thresholds (like revenue milestones, number of customers, etc.), methodically layering in the back-end functions over time to support the growth.

Within the context of this phase, you might be thinking to yourself: what about those functional roles, like accounting, legal, or HR, that aren't necessarily customer-facing nor serving the back-end customer experience post-purchase? Where do they fit into this process?

Remember, every role in a company serves a customer—whether it's your *end-customer* (the ultimate buyer or end-user) or an *internal customer* (like another department or role within the company). These are considered "Cross-functional" roles, and they may serve multiple customers. For example, Accounting might serve the leadership team in preparing month-end financials and cash-flow projections, as well as the customer service team, providing data analysis and accounting around costs and efficiencies.

In addition, they could also serve your new business development person or the marketing manager to prepare contribution margin analysis on customer acquisition. In these instances, a function such as Accounting might serve several different (internal) "customers" and is needed, because it is important to the overall benefit of the company's operations. The role could be minimized, outsourced, or fractional. In other words, it doesn't necessarily need to be a centralized role or in a functional leadership position.

The critical element to filling this position is to focus hiring around the area of greatest impact toward those functions responsible for the business's growth. It's important to find someone with the capabilities that best match this functional need and serve that role.

As you prepare for this leap, the approach to hiring evolves. In a scaling environment, and if the company is limited in its available working capital, the traditional full-time hiring model may not always be the best fit, especially for post startups mindful of their burn rate. Here, the concept of employing "fractional specialists" emerges as a game-changer. There are lots of these professionals in the workforce now who may work part-time or on a contractual basis remotely, and they can often deliver the same level of productivity as a full-time employee but at a fraction of the cost. This can be particularly advantageous in specialized roles where full-time engagement is not necessary or economically feasible.

The value of high-performing talent, at this stage, cannot be understated. According to research by McKinsey & Co., high-performers are up to 400 percent more productive than average employees. This productivity gap widens as roles increase in complexity, with top talent delivering up to 800 percent more productivity in highly specialized positions. Therefore, the strategic use of fractional specialists not only conserves resources but also injects high-quality talent into your organization, catalyzing growth at an even greater velocity.

Phase Three: Now, here's the tricky part: as the company matures (toward Phase III of our Structure), the transition from fractional specialists to a full-fledged leadership team is where the magic of scaling truly happens. It's crucial not to compromise on the quality of these original full-time hires. You need a team of highly talented, highly motivated individuals who not only believe in the company's vision but are also capable of driving it forward.

When in doubt, during the company's *early* stages, I've traditionally found that hiring on EQ (emotional quotient) over IQ (intelligence quotient) is typically the safer bet. The reason is—from research supported by Feist & Barron (1996) and Cherry (2022) as well as our own experiences—higher EQ people tend to get along better with others. They're also better decision-makers, not afraid to ask for help, and are go-getters, driven by this internal curiosity to learn, grow, and figure things out.

In this phase, though, many founders falter, tempted to fill leadership roles hastily. The temptation can be to recruit an "expert" who's been in the industry for decades and seems to have all the answers. Yet, they've only worked inside much larger organizations with much larger teams underneath them.

Instead, the secret is to seek out those who not only have the requisite skills but also a proven track record in dynamic, growth-intensive environments. In other words, they've experienced the growth curve firsthand, working inside a smaller company within the same industry and playing a pivotal role in transforming it into a larger company.

These are intrinsically motivated professionals who thrive under pressure and chaos and won't require large teams or groups of consultants to achieve a high level of performance. These qualities are indispensable in a younger, scaling company. (Do yourself a favor: Please go back and reread this section—it's commonly where we've seen many companies falter and it's worth repeating.)

In summary, building a scale-ready team is a multifaceted process that requires a blend of strategic hiring, insightful leadership development, and an unyielding commitment to the company's core values and vision.

By meticulously planning each step—from the first hire to the mature, experienced leadership team—you lay down the foundation for your business that is not just prepared to scale but destined to thrive inside the imminent chaos of rapid growth.

Evaluating and Attracting the Right People

Jim Collins, a preeminent business thinker whose insights have profoundly influenced my own management strategies, famously stated in his book *Good to Great*, "Great vision without great people is irrelevant." This idea encapsulates the essence of building a successful company—it's about getting the right people on board your company. As an owner or founder, your role transcends the conventional boundaries of management duties. It involves embodying and *selling* your company's vision and its profound aspirational impact to attract world-class talent. This responsibility is intensely personal and cannot be entrusted to a recruiter or HR person, especially when seeking your first hire or forming your initial leadership team. *It needs to come from you.*

The challenge, then, is not just finding talent but finding the right talent—individuals who will drive your vision forward with the same passion and dedication as you. For this purpose, we employ a unique tool: our proprietary Team Impact Evaluator.

This tool is an evolution of the McKinsey 9-box matrix, though it's tailored specifically for dynamic, scaling environments. We've injected a bit of fun into the assessment process. (We think you'll get a laugh out of the creative titles we labeled for each box.) More importantly, we've integrated a critical yet nuanced dimension that often gets overlooked: "cultural fit."

Access The Team Impact Evaluator Tool at ReadyForScaling.com/resources

Cultural fit is a term that's too easily thrown around in the business community. Still, its importance cannot be overstated, especially in the context of a rapidly scaling company. This metric isn't just about ensuring everyone gets along well or has good chemistry. It's about aligning new hires with the core values and operational rhythms of the company. (We'll dive deeper into this subject of operational rhythms in the next chapter.) It's about ensuring everyone is on the same page about what success looks like, how we benefit from those successes, how it should be achieved, and the behaviors and actions most prized by the organization.

This alignment is vital because, throughout the various growth stages of a company, every new addition to your team can significantly sway your culture and operational effectiveness. The wrong people don't just fall short on their performance, they literally pierce the cultural armor and chip away at it, eroding the company's culture you've worked so hard to build. Those aligned with the culture, however, fit not only in terms of skill and experience but in how they embody the spirit of the company—in terms of how they live out the values in their daily tasks and interactions. The right people don't just fulfill their roles; they *enhance* the performance and morale of everyone around them.

Our Team Impact Evaluator helps measure potential candidates against a range of three specific criteria—namely skills growth, expertise, and cultural fit—that are all critically important to your strategic goals and cultural ethos. It goes beyond assessing skills and experience to evaluate how a candidate aligns with the company's mission, their potential for growth, impact on team dynamics, and ability to innovate and drive impact and growth. By placing a measured emphasis on cultural fit, we ensure the dynamism and integrity of your workplace are maintained, even as you scale.

Just as important, this unique tool also plays an important role in evaluating *existing* talent. Often, businesses encounter growth ceilings—whether at $10 million, $25 million, or $50 million in revenue—and struggle to break through. In such cases, our Team Impact Evaluator proves invaluable.

Assuming your strategy and structure are correctly set, we've often uncovered an uncomfortable truth: that is, the talent that helped you reach your current level may not be capable of propelling you to the next. Various factors contribute to this scenario. Perhaps some team member's personal development couldn't keep pace with the company's rapid growth curve. Others might have been overpromoted or overtitled due to early-stage needs. Or, possibly, in the rush of expansion, the leadership team was hastily assembled without thoroughly assessing their ability and cultural adaptability to propel future growth.

Access The Team Impact Evaluator Tool
at ReadyForScaling.com/resources

Necessity of an Internal Talent Audit

During the scaling phases of my previous ventures, I found a great way to start an internal audit of my leadership team by routinely pausing, about every six months, to reflect on a pivotal question: *"Knowing what I know now, would I rehire everyone on my leadership team?"*

If the answer for any member was "no," it highlighted a pressing issue that needed resolution. It's essential not only to evaluate each individual but also to consider the collective influence they wield on your organization's success and their alignment with your company's core values. Reason is, a misaligned leader can wreak havoc and restrict your company's potential to scale, whereas an A-player can dramatically enhance your growth trajectory. We've seen firsthand how the right leadership team member can amplify the overall efforts tenfold.

In fact, in one particularly complex case with a consulting client, a thriving consumer goods company, they had encountered a stubborn revenue ceiling. Our assessment (relying heavily on the Team Impact Evaluation tool) revealed that their leadership team, despite being seasoned and knowledgeable in their respective fields, was paradoxically stifling the company's growth and beginning to erode the company culture.

Addressing this issue with the owner, who also served as CEO, was exceptionally challenging. As consultants, our responsibility is to deliver what our clients need to hear, not necessarily what they wish to hear. This revelation was particularly hard for him to accept, primarily because it required acknowledging flaws in their hiring decisions. We reassured him that these weren't mistakes per se. Rather, they were the best decisions he could have made at the time, given the rapid pace of growth and the information available. Most importantly, we could learn from them. It took about nine months, but we managed to completely revamp and upgrade the leadership team, which included the CFO, CHRO, VP of Legal, VP of Supply Chain, and VP of Compliance & Regulatory. (Needless to say, it was a lot of hard work, though incredibly worthwhile.)

After these changes were implemented, the transformation within the company was profound. It was as if we were working within a completely different entity. The new leadership team fostered a collaborative, goal-driven environment marked by high accountability and performance. This shift was exactly what the company needed to reinstate the dynamic, agile culture that had driven its early success.

Now, if you find yourself uncertain about your feelings toward individuals on your leadership team, here are some deeper questions to guide your evaluation of each member:
- *What is the quality and consistency of their output?*
- *Do they collaborate effectively with their peers?*
- *Are they dedicated to the company's interests above their personal or career ambitions?*
- *How well do they exhibit traits such as humility, a drive for success, and consistent output at a world-class level?*

If you respond negatively to any of these inquiries, you face a choice. Depending, of course, on the number and depth of negative responses you come up with, either terminate and replace the underperforming member or initiate what we refer to as a Rapid Improvement Plan (I know, RIP is a terrible acronym) that's 90 days or less to see improvement in one or several areas identified. This plan sometimes involves reassigning them to roles better suited to their skills. Regardless, the deciding factor for me has always been whether an individual enhances or detracts from the company's culture. If it is a "no," then they must find employment elsewhere.

As the founder, your ability to attract, evaluate, and onboard (or offboard) these individuals will set the foundation for your company's ultimate success and will dictate the rate and level at which it can scale.

Mini Case Study: The "Second Chance" Revolution

When I first stepped into the logistics industry with QuickBox, I was greeted by an unsettling and harsh reality: a nearly 100 percent employee turnover rate in our warehouse operations. Within six months of hiring, we were waving goodbye to practically all our new hires. This wasn't just a drain on resources; it was a blow to morale. I never experienced anything like this in any of my previous companies. And when I asked around to industry pundits, they simply shrugged and told me, "It's the norm; get used to it." I knew there had to be a better way to manage this insane amount of turnover.

The Discovery Walk

Determined to tackle this, I embarked on a journey around QuickBox—called "walking the four corners—a daily practice I learned early on in my role as CEO—where you literally go out, every day, and walk the four corners of the building, stopping to ask questions, learn how people do their jobs, and get to know your employees at a deeper level. My mission was simple yet profound: listen. And listen, I did. From the warehouse floor to the break rooms, I absorbed the stories, the challenges, and the unspoken but common needs of our team.

The Common Thread

Amid these conversations, a pattern emerged. A definitive common thread: that is, I soon discovered many of our most engaged and loyal employees had found themselves in a constant struggle for a fresh start—a chance often unseen or overlooked in the workplace. However, we weren't fully aware that QuickBox was more than just another employer; we were their second chance. By hiring them, we had essentially provided them a "second chance," and in return, these wonderful employees provided QuickBox with their full commitment, loyalty, and hard work.

With this revelation, we pivoted our approach. We reached out to the community, hiring those who needed a second chance the most: recent immigrants, individuals experiencing homelessness, disabled veterans, residents of women's shelters, and those commonly known as the "unemployable," the recently incarcerated. The change was miraculous. Within six months, our retention rate skyrocketed to nearly 70 percent. We continued to lean in further, building additional outreach programs within the surrounding Denver metro areas. Miraculously, we soon discovered we weren't just a logistics company anymore: we had become Colorado's largest second-chance employer.

The Ripple Effect

This initiative did more than just reduce turnover. It created QuickBox's grander mission, injecting a newfound sense of purpose into our work. Our entire company began to rally around this mission—they saw it as the more clients we sign on, the more orders we get to process, therefore the more second chances we get to bring on. Our clients noticed, too. Many partnered with us, not just for our logistics prowess but because they wanted to be part of this transformative journey and contribute to providing these individuals with newfound opportunities. They wanted to join in on our "second chance" mission.

In fact, we changed our tagline to reflect our journey, to "#fulfillmentonamission." By giving a second chance to those who seldom get one, we didn't just transform our business model, we became a mission-driven company through a testament to the power of inclusive employment.

Reflections in Good People

This experience taught me a fundamental lesson: sometimes, the solution to a business challenge isn't in the numbers; it's in the stories and lives of the people who make up your company. And I can tell you, firsthand, nothing—*and I mean nothing*—was so profound and impactful in my life as when an employee would come up to me, shake my hand, and tell me their story, such as how they'd been unhoused, living in Civic Center Park, just six months before and how proud they were to be working for us and thanking me for the second chance to rebuild their life.

These encounters always hit me squarely in the heart and, honestly, make me swell up every time I relive these moments. What's more, I remain friends with many of our past employees and have enjoyed following their continued journeys, even after QuickBox. It brings me great joy and an incredible sense of personal fulfillment to know we played a small part in someone's ability to rebuild their life.

Empower Your Leadership

In the whirlwind of scaling, measuring the effectiveness of your team is not just about tracking numerical outputs but understanding how results are achieved. While we will delve deeper into the specifics of processes, company dashboards, and operational rhythms in the next chapter, it's imperative to establish a foundational under-standing of why the right hires (people) are instrumental in reducing the need for micromanagement and excessive incentivization.

When you align your hiring strategy with the needs of your business and cultural fit, selecting individuals whose capabilities and drive match the demands of their roles, you set the stage for intrinsic motivation to flourish. Great leaders, the kind you want to steer your company's growth, are naturally self-motivated. They are not just participants in your journey. They are co-creators of your enterprise's narrative. Their motivation extends beyond personal gain. I've found it tends to be deeply rooted in the overall success of the organization and the impact of their work.

Let's consider the concept of autonomy, a critical ingredient in fostering an environment where leaders thrive. Autonomy in this context does not mean a lack of direction or oversight but empowering your team within the framework of trust and freedom to execute their responsibilities in the most effective ways. This empowerment is predicated on the belief that the right people, placed in the right roles, bring not only their skills but also their unique perspectives and innovative approaches to solving problems and achieving goals. However, this doesn't imply a completely hands-off approach. The key is to establish clear expectations and success metrics from the start and set up a cadence to check in and measure the progress. Leaders should know what success looks like in their roles and how it aligns with the company's overarching objectives.

Regular check-ins and feedback loops should be part of the rhythm, not to micromanage but to ensure alignment, provide support, and celebrate successes. This balance between guidance and independence allows leaders to feel supported yet free to lead in their style and make decisions that drive the company forward.

While scaling, you especially need leaders to make decisions fast, fail faster (and forward), and continue to improve, which, in theory, should increase the company's operational output. This is called operational velocity. And leaders need to be afforded the benefit of autonomy to carry this out in an environment that doesn't restrict them and instead supports them at this rapid pace.

Moreover, if you've positioned the right leaders, the necessity for external motivators—those proverbial carrots—diminishes. Sure, you can always throw in some vesting equity or company-wide performance bonuses tied to profit.

Regardless of the incentives, though, I've found most high-caliber leaders are driven more by the satisfaction derived from overcoming challenges and achieving significant milestones than by short-term rewards. Their drive is fueled by a vision of what can be accomplished, collectively within the context of a "bigger picture" purpose, and their desire to lead their teams to that end. For them, it's about creating something impactful, something enduring, something that matters.

In fact, this internal drive can be contagious, creating a culture of high performance and continuous improvement throughout the organization. When team members see their leaders pushing boundaries and achieving great results through intrinsic motivation, they are likely to emulate this attitude. This creates a virtuous cycle of motivation and achievement, which is critical in a scaling business where agility and proactive problem-solving are key.

In essence, measuring how results are achieved in a scaling environment involves a blend of strategic hiring, fostering autonomy, and nurturing an intrinsic motivational culture. This approach reduces the reliance on direct oversight and external rewards, instead cultivating a leadership cadre that is self-propelling.

Culture: More Than Just a Buzzword

Ever heard the saying, "Culture eats strategy for breakfast"? While strategy is crucial for scaling, a robust, positive culture is the secret sauce that makes scaling successful and sustainable. It's the difference between a team that merely works for paychecks and one that passionately drives your vision forward.

Let's begin by setting the record straight. Culture isn't the funky artwork on the walls, the quirky traditions on Fridays, or the foosball table in the corner (though those can be fun). It's the collective behavior, values, norms, and shared vision that drive your company forward. It's the invisible hand that guides decisions, actions, and interactions. And I've witnessed culture actually become a competitive advantage, as we'll share in our mini-case study on Smashtech, a vibrant company headed up by two super-driven brothers I've had the pleasure of working with.

The Scaling Culture Conundrum

Somewhere along your journey of scaling, I can say with certainty, you're likely to encounter what I refer to as the "Culture Conundrum." This phenomenon occurs when each new hire, each new office, each new project launch, and each new market entry potentially dilutes the original essence of the company's culture.

Imagine making a cup of coffee: the more creamer you add, the weaker the robustness of the coffee becomes, eventually ruining the flavor. This analogy perfectly encapsulates the challenge of maintaining a robust company culture amidst rapid expansion.

The solution lies not in a laissez-faire attitude of allowing your culture to be built by default but in a deliberate and strategic approach to culture-building. Cultivating culture by design, rather than by haphazard default, is a crucial leadership focus during times of scaling.

This process involves several key conscientious activities. Let's dive into each one of the five:

1. **Defining Core Values**

Clearly establish the values that define your company. These shouldn't be required to live on poster boards surrounding your office. Rather, these are non-negotiable behaviors that everyone from the C-suite to the newest intern must embrace in their heads (and in their hearts). Your values should reflect what is most valued and admired and, equally important, what is not tolerated within the organization.

2. **Hiring and Firing with Values in Mind**

Recruitment and retention must align with these core values. Hire individuals who embody these values, and be prepared to part ways with those who do not. This ensures your team not only performs well but also perpetuates the cultural integrity of your business.

3. **Leading by Example**

As a leader, you are the standard-bearer of your company's culture. "Do as I do *and* as I say," should be the mantra. Your consistent actions, decisions, and communications (verbal and written) set the tone for the rest of the organization, as employees will model their behavior on yours. Inconsistencies between what is said and what is done can erode trust and undermine the cultural foundation.

4. **Overcommunication**

Never underestimate the power of overcommunication. Regularly share stories that highlight your values in action. Recognize and celebrate employees who exemplify these values. Use various platforms, from meetings to internal newsletters to company-wide announcements in Slack, to reinforce the cultural messages. As CEO, I used to write a company-wide update letter religiously each month. In it was a part where we openly shared anecdotal stories of employees getting "caught in the act" of deliberately acting to carry out our values.

5. Maintaining Culture in Adversity

Protecting your cultural values becomes even more critical during tough times. Economic pressures or market downturns might tempt you to cut corners or sideline your cultural agenda for seemingly more immediate gains. However, it is precisely in these moments that your commitment to your values must shine brightest. Scaling back on perks or team events, for instance, should never mean compromising the core behaviors and attitudes that define your organization.

Remember, in the arithmetic of success, your people are the constants; everything else is a variable. By implementing our People principles, you can ensure the talent you've attracted—and the culture you've worked hard to establish—not only survives but thrives even as your company exponentially grows. This proactive approach to talent, leadership, and culture isn't just about preserving the past. It's about building a sustainable future where every new addition strengthens, rather than dilutes, the collective spirit and ethos of your company.

As the leader, it's your role to nurture your talent and mindfully build the culture, ensuring it remains vibrant and cohesive, no matter how turbulent the times or how large your company grows.

Before we dive into the next principle on Process, we encourage you to turn your attention to the story of Smashtech and learn how they've become one of the most desired places to work, even in the midst of massive scaling…

Smashtech: A Mini-Case Study in Building a Culture That's Capable of Enduring Scale

In the world of scaling businesses, one of the most critical yet often overlooked aspects is the preservation and evolution of company culture. As we covered, culture is the heartbeat of a company, the invisible force that drives employee engagement, productivity, and loyalty. To understand the profound impact of culture on a rapidly scaling business, I'd like to turn our attention to the inspiring journey of two brothers—Anwar Imani and Omar Imani—the co-founders of Smashtech, a company I've proudly witnessed firsthand, as our client, since their humble beginnings.

Founded in 2015, Smashtech is a marketing and advertising powerhouse that has grown from a humble start with just $100 and a dream to selling hundreds of millions of dollars in health and wellness products.

Their journey is not just a testament to their business acumen but also to their unwavering commitment to building and maintaining a strong, positive company culture. And as a result, Smashtech has consistently been recognized, more times than I can count, as one of the best places to work in San Diego, thanks to their deliberate, innovative, and empathetic approach to leadership. Here is their story...

The Foundational Principles of Smashtech's Culture

Walk through the doors of Smashtech's headquarters, and it's strikingly easy to see that culture is not a set of contrived policies but an organic extension of the owners' personal values. Anwar and Omar's foundational belief is that business relationships should be treated with the same respect and care as personal relationships. This simple yet profound principle has guided their decisions and policies, such as flexible working hours, unlimited PTO, and a results-oriented work environment.

"We've always prided ourselves on doing things differently," Anwar explains. "We trust our employees to manage their time and responsibilities. Respect and autonomy lead to higher productivity and satisfaction. We wanted to create an environment where people look forward to coming to work, similar to how we take pride in our homes."

Tactical Strategies for Fostering Positive Culture

From the inception of Smashtech, Anwar and Omar implemented several tactical strategies to foster a positive workplace culture. These strategies were not based on corporate textbooks but on their gut instincts and a strong sense of empathy and respect. They emphasized the power of proximity and in-person collaboration, believing that working closely together fosters a sense of community and accelerates problem-solving.

"Our approach has always been organic," Anwar says. "We've never viewed culture as something to be contrived in a boardroom. Instead, we focused on creating a space that felt like a family-oriented dynamic because we genuinely are family. This approach has resonated with our employees and contributed to our success."

Smashtech's Recognition and the Key Factors

Smashtech's exceptional culture has earned them numerous awards as one of the best places to work. Anwar attributes this consistent recognition to their deep understanding of human relationships. "It's about making sure people feel seen, heard, and understood," he explains. "We personalize our interactions and genuinely care about our team members. Our culture of empathy, respect, and transparency has been pivotal."

Challenges and Preservation of Cultural Values

Scaling a business comes with its challenges, and Smashtech has faced its share. One of the significant challenges was managing rapid growth while preserving their cultural values. Anwar recounts a time when they were strapped for cash and couldn't afford to give raises or make additional cultural investments.

"During these tough times, radical transparency was key," Anwar excitedly says. "We communicated openly about our financial situation and the long-term vision. This honesty helped maintain trust and unity within the team. It was critical to stay true to our values, even when it was difficult."

Finding "Cultural Fit" While Hiring and Integrating New Employees

Hiring the right people is imperative for maintaining culture during rapid growth. At Smashtech, the focus is on intangible qualities like empathy, respect, and a willingness to learn. "Skill sets can be taught, but core values are essential," Anwar emphasizes. "We look for people who align with our values and can integrate into our culture seamlessly."

Once hired, new employees are integrated through a supportive environment where servant leadership is practiced. "Our leadership team works hard to serve and support the entire organization, ensuring everyone feels valued and aligned with our cultural values," Anwar explains.

Impact on Extraordinary Business Outcomes

"Our culture has a direct impact on our business outcomes," proclaims Anwar. Smashtech's commitment to a strong company culture has significantly enhanced both productivity and retention. By treating everyone with empathy and respect and fostering a supportive environment, they've created a workplace where people want to stay and thrive. This approach has led to higher levels of engagement and loyalty among their employees. Anwar goes on to say, "When employees feel valued and supported, they are more productive and committed to the company's success."

Interestingly, Smashtech doesn't rely on formal feedback mechanisms to measure the success of its cultural initiatives. Instead, they gauge cultural health through the organic feel and spirit of the company. Honest conversations and radical transparency are key. "When things are going well, you can see it in the external recognition and awards we receive, as well as in the overall internal morale of the team," Anwar explains. "It's about maintaining an open dialogue and being attuned to the needs and feelings of our employees."

The Evolution of Smashtech's Culture

As Smashtech has grown, the culture has evolved, particularly in terms of transparency. Initially, there were many one-off conversations, but the owners realized the importance of sharing information company-wide. This increased transparency has helped elevate their culture, making everyone feel more included and informed.

"We've radically increased levels of transparency as we've grown," Anwar says. "It dawned on me that I was having so many one-off conversations with key stakeholders. Now, we share valuable information with the entire company. This approach has strengthened our culture tremendously."

Anwar firmly believes that Smashtech's culture is a competitive advantage. "In the marketing and advertising space, it's hard to attract and retain top talent," he explains. "Our strong culture sets us apart. It helps us build better relationships with customers and drives our success. If I didn't own Smashtech, I would still want to work here because of the positive and supportive culture we've built."

Future Plans and New Initiatives

Looking to the future, Smashtech plans to continue investing in their employees' personal and professional development. One exciting initiative is bringing in mental coaches for their team. Inspired by the performance coaches seen in the TV show *Billions*, these coaches, in a one-on-one environment, will help employees navigate personal and professional challenges, ensuring they are mentally strong and fully engaged at work.

"Investing in mental health and well-being is a natural extension of our commitment to supporting our team," Anwar explains. "It's about helping our employees be their best selves, both personally and professionally."

Smashtech's journey is a powerful example of how a strong, empathetic, and transparent culture can drive business success, especially during rapidly scaling growth and even in the most challenging times. By treating business relationships with the same care and respect as personal ones, Anwar and Omar have built a company where people are genuinely excited to work, fostering an environment of trust, loyalty, and high performance.

In the end, the lesson from Smashtech's story is clear: *culture is not a set of policies but a way of life*. It's about creating a

supportive environment where everyone feels valued, respected, and empowered to succeed.

- Keller, Scott. Focus on the Five Percent. McKinsey & Co.

- https://www.mckinsey.com/capabilities/people-and-organizational-per-
formance/our-insights/the-organization-blog/focus-on-the-five-percent

- Cherry, K. (2022a). 7 Habits of emotionally intelligent people. *Very Well Mind.* https://www.verywellmind.com/the-7-habits-of-emotionally-in-telligent-people-2795431

- Feist, G., & Barron, F. (1996). *Emotional intelligence and academic intelligence in career and life success.* Annual Convention of the American Psychological Society 1996, San Francisco, CA.

Chapter 8

Process—The Backbone of Efficient Scaling

I'll never forget: during a pivotal meeting with a prospective buyer for QuickBox, our logistical order fulfillment company, we were asked with a smirk, "Do you have an SOP for going to the bathroom?" This query, while humorous, highlighted our deep commitment to precision through process engineering in *every* facet of our operations.

At QuickBox, our daily operations involved managing hundreds of thousands of inventory items that belonged to our clients which would be assembled in individual outgoing packages. On many days, this was over 30,000 orders. Having an abundance of processes wasn't just a matter of organizational pride; it was essential. The nature of our business demanded that every process be repeatable, sustainable, documented, and meticulously crafted to maximize throughput velocity while minimizing error rates. This stringent requirement for clearly defined SOPs (standard operating procedures) was not about bureaucratic overreach but about building a robust foundation that could handle massive scale without faltering or making errors.

As we grew in volume and matured as a company, we embraced systems automation, which enhanced our operational scaling efficiency further. We thought of this evolution as the "multiplier effect." Ultimately, it was what allowed our team to shift focus from repetitive tasks to strategic decision-making. (We'll cover systems in greater detail later in this chapter.)

Now, that said, it's essential to acknowledge that not every business will require the same level of detailed process management as we did at QuickBox. The nature of your business, the industry you operate in, and the scale at which you work will dictate the functional areas of the company and the extent to which detailed processes are necessary.

However, the principle remains universally applicable: clear, well-documented processes—and an overarching management operating system—are the backbone of scalability. They provide a framework that supports growth, ensures consistency in product or service delivery, and builds confidence among stakeholders—from employees and management to customers and even investors.

Why Documentation Matters

When we step into a company for the first time, one of our initial tasks is to review processes. Surprisingly often, we find that these processes exist primarily in one place, the worst possible place: *a single person's head.* This scenario, as you can imagine, poses a significant risk. If that person were to unexpectedly leave, be promoted, or even get hit by a bus, the company could be left scrambling to re-engineer essential processes from scratch. In addition, if processes only live inside one's head, the company will struggle to ever achieve scale.

Knowing this, it is time to pull up your big-kid britches, extract those processes out of their (or your) head, and put them on paper. Documenting these procedures is not just about preservation. It's the first step toward optimizing them and your business. By simply translating tacit knowledge into explicit, actionable instructions, according to a recent study, companies often experience an immediate and profound improvement in operational efficiency.

Skeptical? Try it with a process inside your business and see the immediate difference it makes not only in day-to-day operations but also in critical transition periods like delegating work and especially when boarding a new employee.

Ultimately, if improving your day-to-day operations isn't enticing enough, having standardized processes documented is a necessity if you ever decide to sell your business. Buyers aren't just purchasing your brand, products, or services; they're buying your operational standardization. They want to know that the business can run effectively *without* the founder's hands-on involvement. Standardizing and documenting your processes solidify the company's operating structure, making it more attractive to buyers and typically increasing its overall enterprise value.

Access The Process Builder at ReadyForScaling.com/resources: It's faster and easier to visualize and document with our pre-built prompts.

Scaling Without Sacrificing Quality

One of the keys to sustainable scaling for any business is doing so without sacrificing the quality of your product or service. This is where process development and continuous improvement become cornerstones to deliver on your brand's promise. In their simplest form, processes are a systematic series of actions directed to achieve a specific outcome. These procedures are crucial for scaling because they ensure consistency and efficiency across operations, enabling any business to handle increased volumes without sacrificing quality, compliance, or control.

By setting clear guidelines and expectations, processes allow for consistent operational throughput during periods of growth and change, ensuring all team members are aligned and that the operations can scale up without significant hitches or decreased quality. In addition, and perhaps more importantly, processes allow for the delegation of key functions, resulting in less involvement in day-to-day hands-on management and enhanced organizational trust.

Identifying and developing robust processes in key operational areas is crucial for overcoming the initial inertia of managing your business beyond its startup phase while minimizing the entropy—a naturally occurring state of disorder and inefficiency within the business that accompanies growth. Without structured processes, the transitional growth periods can be marred with inefficiencies and delays, akin to trying to build a skyscraper without blueprints and engineering plans. This lack of clarity and direction can quickly sap any initial momentum and enthusiasm necessary to get your business's operational flywheel turning.

As your business expands, the significance of these processes becomes even more critical. Growth introduces complexity, which proportionally increases the likelihood of entropy. Without well-defined processes in key areas that drive your strategy (such as new business development, customer acquisition, product development, customer service, and inventory management), your operations can, and will, struggle to maintain consistency and quality and fail to scale. This struggle can also result in errors and inefficiencies that stall growth and frustrate both your employees and your customers.

In theory, or from the sidelines, it might seem like every operational aspect demands its own SOP or detailed process. In practice, though, we've found that focusing your efforts primarily on *key driver areas* can yield the most substantial returns. Although numerous aspects of a company's operations could potentially benefit from stringent processes, you must be selective because poorly managed processes—or not having a defined process altogether—can wreak havoc on the operations and will inevitably become constraints. Thus, prioritization of key processes is essential.

To streamline your approach to process generation and ensure effective scaling, we typically concentrate on three major areas:

(i) Key Function Identification;
(ii) Operational Rhythm; and
(iii) Company Dashboard.

Let's dive into each of these...

Process Area I: Identifying Key Processes that Drive Business Productivity

In the earlier stages of scaling a business, we've found it's vital to discern which processes genuinely propel your company forward versus those that are secondary supporting functions. This is the first critical step in enhancing productivity as, while every business has multiple functions if you look closely enough, studying the entire value chain of your complete business cycle, only a select few processes are actually pivotal in driving growth or increasing output (preferably those which contribute to growth).

For example, if you're a consumer goods company, your customer acquisition or inventory procurement and planning processes might be key. Whereas for a software company, your key processes could be the product development lifecycle or new customer onboarding. (These key processes are likely executed by the teams you identified earlier while covering the chapter on Structure.)

To start, conduct a thorough analysis of your current operational value chain. Then, pinpoint areas where an improvement to throughput or standardization could yield disproportionately large benefits. This might involve streamlining supply chain logistics or automating customer service responses. The goal is to focus on processes that, when optimized, directly boost productivity and contribute to your bottom line through efficiency or top line through growth. Implementing SOPs in these areas ensures your team performs these tasks efficiently and consistently, leading to predictable and improved business outcomes.

Remember, the key isn't to complicate your business but to simplify and fortify the processes that matter most to execute your strategy and drive growth.

Mini-Case Study: Enhancing Productivity Around Core Competencies

As an example of how this plays out, in a recent consulting project for a consumer-packaged goods company, we encountered a typical challenge: the organization was mired in giving equal attention to every operational aspect, a common stumbling block in the transition from moving past the startup phase and into scaling. In this scenario, it's easy to imagine your business as a series of spinning plates, each requiring equally consistent attention to prevent disaster. However, our experience has shown that this perception often leads to over-managing and inefficiencies.

Our first step was to pinpoint the company's core strengths and competencies, which were product development, marketing, and an intense focus on customer satisfaction. Despite these strengths, we discovered that the company was getting bogged down with in-house manufacturing and order fulfillment. At the same time, their marketing was outsourced to a top-rated agency that, unfortunately, paid them very little attention (or at least it felt that way).

To streamline their operations and enhance scalability, we recommended a strategic realignment of their key activities to match their internal talents, capabilities, and core competencies. This involved a significant shift: moving away from in-house manufacturing and order fulfillment, which were distractions from their core competencies, and bringing the marketing activities in-house to better align with their capabilities.

The transition was structured in stages over six months to minimize disruption, as businesses can only absorb so much change at once. We outsourced their manufacturing to very capable co-manufacturers who could maintain quality and pricing, transitioned to a bicoastal third-party logistics provider for warehousing and order fulfillment, and took control of the marketing internally. This integration allowed for a better alignment with their strategic goals and organizational structure (which had just undergone reorganization).

By narrowing the focus of process development to its core competency and capability strengths, the company could then further enhance and control the key growth-driving functions. We optimized the product development process to launch new products more frequently, which would keep them at the forefront of market innovation. Marketing efforts, now handled internally, were aligned more closely with the company's brand and strategic goals, simultaneously expanding their reach and engagement with customers. Additionally, we upgraded their customer service by recruiting top-tier leadership talent and implemented automated systems to enhance service delivery and scalability.

Once these changes were fully implemented, the company was not only aligned more closely with its strengths and capabilities but also positioned robustly for scalable growth. This strategic realignment—and supplementary process design—allowed them to focus on what they do best, setting the stage for sustained success.

Process Area II: Establishing an Effective Battle Rhythm

We find that communication is the lifeblood of any growing organization, and establishing a solid battle rhythm through regular meetings is essential for maintaining this flow. These scheduled interactions are not just for updates but are strategic avenues for facilitating decision-making and problem-solving across all levels of the organization. By setting a consistent schedule for meetings—whether daily stand-ups, weekly departmental check-ins, or monthly all-hands—everyone stays informed, aligned, and accountable.

The key is to ensure these meetings are productive and focused. Hearing this, I'm sure you might be saying to yourself, *"But our company can't handle another meeting!"* While that might be true, our experiences have told us that half of the meetings in your company, right now, could likely be eliminated, and you wouldn't miss a beat.

However, when a meeting is structured with an intentional purpose and stated outcome and is tracked in a system that allows for quick and efficient follow-up (we'll touch on this later in systems), these meetings can and will drive the rhythm and speed of growth with faster and more deliberate decision-making and problem-solving. In essence, the frequency of your meetings will increase the rate of your company's ability to scale.

And what happens as a result of building a frequent cadence of deliberate meetings? You will out-execute your competitors. And this, my friend, can become a serious competitive advantage.

The meetings should serve as platforms for cross-functional communication, enabling teams to synchronize their efforts and maintain alignment. In these settings, leadership can offer guidance around prioritization or help resolve issues where people or business units find themselves stuck on unsolved problems. Effective meeting rhythms help prevent silos and ensure that information moves both vertically and laterally throughout the organization.

This regular cadence of communication helps identify bottlenecks early, align priorities, and reinforce the company's strategic objectives, thereby fostering a cohesive environment that's ready to scale.

The Amplified Power of the Daily Standup

Let's take a look at how we established an effective, purposeful battle rhythm in an organization. At QuickBox, managing multiple warehouses across various states and overseeing more than 500 employees, one might assume there was no time for regular meetings. Yet, it was precisely the operational rhythm that allowed the structured communication vital to our ability to scale so rapidly. Akin to the adage about sharpening the saw before cutting down the tree, a small bit of preparation makes the task much more efficient. In other words, preparation drives performance.

We implemented a straightforward, transparent communications operating system documented in OneNote (part of Microsoft's Office suite), which proved easy to manage for everyone at every level of the company. Crucially, every business unit throughout the entire organization conducted a daily stand-up planning meeting, seven days a week, year-round. And every meeting was documented.

These meetings ensured alignment on our "daily plans" and allowed us to monitor progress more easily throughout the day. This regular check-in enabled us to adjust to unforeseen circumstances or flex labor dynamically and ensure our ultimate operational goal: 100 percent of client orders fulfilled each day.

Communication flowed consistently from these daily meetings into weekly team meetings, held by each business unit, where each unit reported updates and issues. Every other week, team leaders gathered for a leadership meeting to exchange information and data as well as make strategic decisions. Insights and data from these meetings were then channeled back to their respective teams.

The culmination of this structured communication process was our weekly executive meeting, where outputs from each business unit were reviewed. We structured these executive meetings to optimize our focus on digesting operational performance quickly, which then allowed us to shift our discussion to broader strategic issues and initiatives.

This rhythm of meetings was vigorously maintained, requiring minimal oversight yet offering maximum transparency, accountability, and throughput. This critical process—along with our discipline to uphold it—allowed us not only to manage day-to-day operations effectively but also to respond swiftly to any challenges, keeping leadership focused on executing the overarching strategy and driving transformational efforts to expand the business. Ultimately, I believe, it was a competitive advantage for our business that allowed us to outproduce our competitors.

Process Area III: The Ultimate Performance Feedback Loop: A Simple, Effective Company Dashboard

A well-designed company dashboard is imperative for monitoring the health of your business. It translates complex data into early warning signs and actionable insights and focuses on Key Performance Indicators (KPIs) that align with the critical processes identified earlier. The simplicity of the dashboard is key. It should provide immediate clarity, be limited to only the key functions, and allow not just decision-makers but everyone in the company to gauge performance at a glance. The aim is to foster a data-driven culture where strategic decisions are grounded in facts and figures, not hope, intuition, or dangerous assumptions.

The adage *"what gets measured gets managed"* holds particularly true in the context of business scaling. For many of our clients, thankfully, some form of company-wide data reporting and distribution is often already in place, and that's a commendable start. At the initial stages of growth, simplicity in data management is key. There are numerous software options available for tracking and distributing data, which we'll explore in the next section. Still, the primary takeaway here is the critical importance of aligning the company around key data, having transparent accountability, and using this data to make informed decisions.

To develop an effective dashboard, we begin by identifying Key Performance Indicators (KPIs) that mirror the health and efficiency of a company's primary business drivers. Our approach is to select no more than three KPIs for each main function and one KPI for all other secondary functions. For instance, with our consumer-packaged goods (CPG) clients, where customer acquisition and product trial are critical metrics, the KPIs might include traffic source quantity, conversion rates, and average cost per acquisition.

In areas like inventory planning, key metrics could be inventory turns, days on hand, and GMROI (gross margin return on investment). For customer experience, we often track metrics such as Net Promoter

Score (NPS), cumulative online reviews, and customer refunds. Once primary functions are adequately covered, we move to secondary areas such as technology, finance, people, products, and legal or compliance. We ask the business unit leaders to select one primary metric for their respective functions.

After each business unit has its unique KPIs identified, we work closely with the leadership team to have them select *the single* metric that best represents the company's highest strategic goal. Yes, *just one*. As difficult as this is to agree on, its significance cannot be understated. This metric should be a comprehensive indicator of the company's overall health, and direction, at any given time.

For example, one of our CPG clients in the pet supplement market chose "number of orders per day" as this metric, providing a reliable measure of the business's health and alignment toward its primary strategic target. Because they were well aware of the average order value, cost to serve the customer order, and the expected lifetime value of the customer, this metric (orders per day) served as a predictive indicator of the company's current and future health and, cumulatively, whether it was on course with its financial performance. We highly encourage leaders to identify and elevate this "one thing"—a metric that encapsulates your company's most important performance indicator—ensuring it is visible company-wide and frequently reviewed and discussed.

The Importance of KPIs

The significance of KPIs in driving business decisions and operations cannot be overstated. Relying solely on financial statements to guide business decisions is often inadequate; these reports are usually retrospective and become available days after the month's end, potentially too late for responsive action. This traditional form of reporting, while important for stakeholders like banks and shareholders, does not offer the agility needed in today's fast-paced business environments.

Conversely, a dashboard equipped with real-time KPIs provides a dynamic overview of a company's operations, allowing for timely decision-making and agile responses to market changes or inefficiencies within the company. This proactive approach to data management enables businesses to pivot strategies more swiftly without severe repercussions, such as unnecessary cash burn or operational disruptions. By managing to this real-time data, leaders can effectively steer their companies—making informed decisions quickly and maintaining operational continuity without compromising any part of the business. This level of responsiveness is a priority for scaling businesses.

Building the Optimal Management Operating System

As you integrate the key processes you've pinpointed, solidify your battle rhythm, and align these with your most vital KPIs, you're well on your way to establishing a robust management operating system. This juncture is where many companies stumble. They make the process of an operating system overly complex. Or worse, they're completely absent of one. There's often a tendency to adopt an operating system that is too cumbersome, leading to poor adoption and eventual disuse, erasing all the hard work invested in setting it up.

Instead, once you have laid the groundwork, choose a technology solution that seamlessly displays and tracks the rhythm of your company's operations. At QuickBox, we opted for a simple yet effective tool from Microsoft Office: OneNote. However, the tools you might consider could range from Google Sheets (or Excel) to more specialized software like Monday.com or Trello.

I'm frequently asked about the optimal tool for managing an operating system. My response harks back to advice I would give during my days in the fitness industry. When asked which home gym equipment to buy, my answer was always the same: *choose the equipment you're most likely to use.* The same principle applies to your management operating system. Select a tool that you—and your team—are most likely to engage with consistently. The success of your operating system doesn't hinge on the sophistication of the technology but on its usability and the disciplined frequency with which your team uses it to stay aligned, track progress, and drive the company forward.

For scaling businesses, the ability to make quick, data-informed decisions and maintain frequent, structured communication is often a common denominator in successful scaling stories. That's why it's crucial to adopt a system that fits naturally with your business culture and operational needs—forcing an ill-fitting system can be more detrimental than beneficial. Thus, choose an operating system that supports swift decision-making and fosters regular, meaningful interactions. Remember, the best systems are those that you're more prone to use and will ultimately enhance your ability to act on reliable data and maintain the operational rhythm essential for efficient scaling.

Software: Pouring Fuel on the Fire with Tech

When considering the structure of business operations, it's important to distinguish between processes and systems. At its core, a process involves a series of steps and actions taken to achieve a specific outcome. A system, on the other hand, can be seen as leverage—a tool that supports and automates these processes to enhance efficiency and output without proportionally increasing resource allocation.

In the realm of scaling businesses, systems often manifest as software-as-a-service (SaaS) technology. SaaS solutions provide a remarkable advantage by automating various business operations, allowing companies to scale their capabilities without necessarily increasing their headcount. There's literally a SaaS for almost every component of a business's operations. This shift in how businesses operate has dramatically transformed the economic landscape. For instance, today, we consult with clients who generate between $25 and $50 million in annual revenue and operate efficiently with only 8 to 15 employees. This is a stark contrast to the early 2000s—when

I began my entrepreneurial journey—where achieving similar revenue figures typically required a workforce of 25 to 50 people.

This efficiency is largely dependent on the business model, but for a vast majority of companies, SaaS technologies serve as a powerful tool for achieving scalable growth. These software solutions act as accelerants, speeding up operations, reducing the need for manual input, and allowing businesses to expand their reach and capabilities more rapidly than ever before through automation. By integrating SaaS into your core operations, you can leverage this technology to drive growth, enhance productivity, and maintain a lean workforce, at scale.

After having the luxury of working with hundreds of companies across a diverse range of industries and business models—from direct-to-consumer and Amazon to mass-market retail distribution—we have had the privilege of gaining a comprehensive overview of their operational systems. This bird's-eye view has allowed us to observe a spectrum of operational efficiencies. And while a few companies were poorly managed, the large majority were well-oil operations equipped with sophisticated software systems that bolstered their scaling capabilities.

Countless hours of diligent scrutiny of various business operations have revealed insights into which technologies truly enhance functionality and which ones fail to deliver on their promises or, worse, divert focus and resources. This extensive evaluation has led to the identification of the *most* effective software solutions tailored to specific aspects of business operations. Whether it's boosting marketing effectiveness, streamlining human resources and payroll, automating customer service, or reducing shipping costs, the focus has always been on selecting technologies with substantive value. These efforts have not only clarified which solutions are truly beneficial but have also helped save these companies millions, dropping enhanced operational income straight to their bottom lines.

Recognizing that the landscape of technology is continuously evolving—with innovations emerging and older systems being replaced—we've committed ourselves to staying abreast of these changes. We continually assess new technologies against established ones to determine their efficacy and practicality. When a new system proves superior, outperforming its predecessors, we do not hesitate to embrace it and recommend its adoption to our clients. This proactive approach ensures that the businesses we advise are always at the cutting edge, equipped with the best tools to facilitate their growth and enhance their operational efficiency.

Access our free download for The Ultimate Software Technologies, listing the top SaaS technologies for scaling businesses at ReadyForScaling.com/resources.

Integrating software strategically and efficiently is crucial for scaling businesses effectively. When working with clients, our approach to technology integration is tailored based on their stage in the revenue cycle and specific business needs. For example, if your company is further along on its revenue path (into the eight figures), our focus is on identifying key functions or strategic priorities that are critical for growth. We then explore how these can be optimized with technology to enhance performance and efficiency or automation.

For businesses at an earlier stage of revenue growth (sub $10 million), our strategy differs slightly. We begin at the customer interface, constructing an ecosystem of software solutions designed to enhance the customer journey from initial engagement through to purchase, fulfillment, inventory management, and post-purchase support. This method ensures the technology not only improves the buying experience but also boosts revenue metrics and streamlines inventory management.

Regardless of the company's stage, the overarching goal with software systems is to achieve the greatest efficiency for the investment made—i.e., getting the "biggest bang for your buck." This principle is exemplified in our mini-case study of the Obvi supplement company, where targeted software investments significantly propelled their business operations and have allowed them to successfully scale.

More recently, with one direct-to-consumer consumer goods client in particular, our process involved carefully prioritizing the business's needs and integrating each new technology solution systematically. We ensured that each tool was fully integrated and rigorously tested and that staff were well-trained and comfortable using it before moving on to the next software solution. This methodical approach, which we advise for those deploying new software, avoids the pitfalls of over-complicating the system architecture prematurely and allows the company to experience the enhancements of the system in a more controlled environment.

Eventually, they built out a complete customer engagement and support system of tools that allowed them to dramatically enhance revenue without adding a single additional employee. By focusing on securing quick wins in optimization, we maintained momentum and clarity throughout the technology integration phases.

Ultimately, this approach results in a cohesive architecture of systems, each contributing to the operational connectivity and velocity of the business. Through automated enhancements, this setup propels the company toward scalable growth, ensuring every technology investment moves the business significantly closer to achieving its scaling objectives.

However, the real risk in integrating technological (SaaS) systems isn't necessarily in the technology itself failing to perform. Rather, it's in not fully leveraging these tools to their maximum potential in your business. If you, as an entrepreneur, don't use the systems you've invested in, you risk missing crucial efficiencies that could truly revolutionize how your business operates.

Therefore, the key challenge is not simply adopting new technology but deeply integrating and optimizing these systems within your company. Doing so ensures you're not just keeping pace with industry developments but are also leveraging technological advancements to your competitive advantage. Make no mistake, this approach will secure the substantial benefits that technology offers, helping your business scale more effectively and sustainably faster.

Access a comprehensive list of our vetted SaaS by business function at ReadyForScaling.com/resources.

Now, before we delve into our next principle—Cash—you don't want to miss out on learning how our good friends at Obvi, a leading health and wellness supplement brand, are one of the better companies we've ever witnessed in leveraging technology to propel their hyper-fast-growing business.

Leveraging Technology to Scale: The Obvi Case Study

In the ever-evolving landscape of health and wellness, Obvi has carved an impressive niche by specializing in collagen-based supplements. Founded by Ronak Shah, Ashvin Melwani, and Ankit Patel, Obvi stands out not only for its innovative products but also for its strategic use of technology to scale efficiently. The brand's commitment to transparency, quality, and customer engagement has driven it to surpass $40 million in annual sales and is well on their way to $100 million. This success, in no small part, is a direct result of their meticulous approach to technology and systems.

To take a closer look under the hood, I talked with long-time friend and CEO of Obvi, Ronak ("Ron") Shah, who shared valuable insights into how technology can be harnessed to enhance your business's processes and support scaling efforts.

Adopting Technology with a Strategic Mindset

At the core of Obvi, technology is seen as a practical application of knowledge, aimed at enhancing the business's growth and success. "We aim for simplicity in integrating technology," Ronak explains. This straightforward approach ensures that technology serves its purpose *without* complicating the operations.

Ron goes on to explain, "At Obvi, the primary aim of technology adoption is to achieve efficiency, saving both time and money." Emphasizing, "Our guiding principle is continuous improvement, ensuring we never become stagnant or complacent." This relentless pursuit of efficiency has kept Obvi at the forefront of their competitive market.

Technology Is Not a Panacea

From day one, Obvi's ownership team views technology as an enhancer, or multiplier per se, of their capabilities rather than a "cure-all solution." Effective technology should aid in operational efficiency and facilitate a more personal connection with customers—both internal and external. "We view technology not as a panacea but as an enhancer of our capabilities," Ron notes, highlighting the strategic role technology plays in their operations.

When determining where technology can produce the biggest impact, Obvi focuses on bandwidth. They assess whether a tool or program can perform tasks faster and with equal or better quality than manual methods. This approach allows them to allocate more time to their strengths and specialties. "Our decision-making revolves around bandwidth," says Ron. This pragmatic approach ensures that technology investments are justified by tangible, ROI-driven paybacks or improvements in efficiency and quality.

Avoiding Integration Flops

The really smart approach Obvi takes for a successful integration of any new technology hinges on a clear understanding of their daily business operations and all affected stakeholders. Obvi identifies where technology can fill gaps in efficiency, automation, or profitability. "Integration success hinges on self-awareness and a clear understanding of everyone's role in its adoption," Ron points out. This self-awareness enables Obvi to migrate and adopt new technologies most effectively.

The reason Obvi goes to great lengths to ensure its integrations are seamless is because, as most of us have experienced, new technologies can disrupt existing processes, even cripple companies. But Obvi mitigates these risks by reviewing past case studies, surveying user reviews, and closely monitoring performance, especially during critical times of its early adoption. And, to ensure that new tech tools or systems support their ROI objectives, Obvi sets measurable KPIs up front, before deployment. If a tool under-performs, they consider extending timelines, adjusting parameters, or revising target KPIs. "Adaptability is key in managing these risks," says Ron.

Successful Technology Integration

Obvi's customer experience (CX) automation with Gorgias is a prime example of successful technology integration. This automation allows them to efficiently manage up to 5,000 customer tickets monthly with less than two full-time staff members. "Our customer experience automation with Gorgias showcases the power of automation in maintaining high-quality CX, even with a lean team," Ron highlights.

Additionally, software tools like AfterSell and Proxima have significantly enhanced Obvi's revenue and marketing performance. AfterSell helped them achieve a $4.80 lift in revenue per transaction, translating to an 11 percent increase in average order value (AOV) in just two weeks, enabling them to scale Meta ad spend by +2.3x.

Obvi's story is a testament to the power of leveraging technological advancements to enhance systems and processes to create massive efficiencies. With the right operational backbone through technological systems, even the less experienced, understaffed, or ambitious entrepreneurs can compete and win in a highly competitive arena.

Obvi's insights provide a valuable blueprint for those looking to harness technology in the scaling journey, emphasizing the importance of strategic adoption, continuous improvement, and effective integration.

Conclusion

As we wrap up our exploration of processes, systems, and the technology that make them more efficient, it's essential to recognize their transformative potential in scaling your business. Clearly defined and documented processes, a transparent management operating system, along with the right technology, can streamline your operations, enhance efficiency, improve communications, and accelerate your growth, giving you a serious competitive edge, especially if the tech stack is put together thoughtfully and strategically.

So now that we've covered Strategy, Structure, People, and Processes, how do we fuel your growth? With capital, of course. Let's dive into our next, and final principle—Cash…

https://www.ncbi.nlm.nih.gov/pmc/articles/PMC4639364/

Chapter 9

Cash—The Fuel for Your Scaling Endeavor

I'll never forget: after our company went public in 2012, during our inaugural board meeting, the Chairman (and largest shareholder) Russell Cleveland, who embodied the archetype of a seasoned business leader with his stern demeanor and insightful gaze, leaned across the conference table and said to me in a gruff voice, *"I've got two rules. If you can follow them, we'll get along just fine. Rule number one, never run out of cash. Number two, never forget rule number one."*

Although his delivery had a touch of humor, the gravity of his words resonated deeply. Indeed, cash is no laughing matter. In a scaling

company, as the great management guru Peter Drucker so elo-
quently said, "growth eats cash for breakfast, lunch, and dinner"
(and I add, sometimes even dessert).

In this chapter, we're going to delve into the critical role of cash—not
just profits or operating income (which are undeniably crucial to sustainable growth) but the flow of cash. We'll explore examples of effective cash management strategies, emphasizing how well-struc-
tured financial practices can fuel your company's growth *internally*.
We're going to examine a few financial ratios that are vitally important to understand before embarking on scaling. Finally, we'll
cover scenarios where tapping into external funding becomes necessary by looking closely at how to calculate your business's capital
needs to support scale—*without running out of cash.*

As you'll soon discover, intimately understanding and managing cash
flow is paramount, as it not only ensures operational stability but also
secures your company's path to scaling up sustainably. In fact, out of
all factors, running out of cash is the number one reason why businesses fail, accounting for 82 percent of businesses shutting down.

The perils of inadequate cash planning, insufficient capital to support hyper-growth, or mismanagement of funds top the list of reasons why companies falter and ultimately close their doors. In essence, you should think of cash as your oxygen. Cut it off or run out
of it, and you die.

As a business founder, imagine, for a moment, waking up to discover you can't make payroll that week. You might think this scenario is unlikely, but I have personally experienced it (and it literally made me vomit), as have countless other businesses. It's a dreadful situation—one that underscores the vital importance of masterful cash management.

Fortunately, you don't need to be a CFO or CPA to master these financial concepts. Later in this chapter, we'll introduce an exceptional tool we crafted, called The 7 Levers Cash Navigator, that simplifies the concepts underlying the management of cash flow optimization—a resource I wish had been available during the early stages of my entrepreneurial journey.

This tool was designed to demystify financial concepts and equip you with a practical look into what precisely is needed, can be initiated, and should be prioritized to optimize your company's cash flow. It's an invaluable asset for any founder looking to confidently and strategically navigate the challenges of scaling a business with financial foresight.

This chapter also underscores the final, critical principle in scaling your business—understanding how much cash is needed to support scale *while* mastering your cash flow. A sound understanding of cash management will not only help you avoid the terminal diagnosis of financial insolvency but also empower you to navigate growth phases with confidence and resilience and, if done well, internally finance your growth.

Rather than over-complicate matters related to responsible cash management and fiscal stewardship, when we engage with clients, we typically concentrate our efforts on two or three key areas:

(i) Drilling Down on Cash Flow Forecasting,

(ii) Mastering the Cash Conversion Cycle,

(iii) Estimating Your Growth Capital Needs and, if necessary, seeking external funding.

By focusing on these critical aspects, we can streamline our approach to ensure effective management of financial resources, maintaining clarity and control over your cash flow processes.

We've found this targeted approach helps uncover the hidden and sometimes uncomfortable truths about the company's fiscal prudence, ultimately optimizing the financial operations to support the company's growth momentum.

Financial Cash Management: Looking Around the Corner

Assuming you already have accurate and regularly updated monthly financial statements like an income statement and balance sheet, we can shift our attention to a crucial component that's often and too easily overlooked: a cash flow projection tool (emphasis on the word *projection*). This tool should not merely be a statement of cash flows but a dynamic, regularly reviewed projection—ideally assessed at least weekly, sometimes daily, and no less frequently than monthly.

The determining factor for the frequency of review is the speed and volatility of your business's operations. Honestly, if you don't have a cash projection tool in place, you've lost the race before it even started. Financial cash management transcends the simple tracking of income and expenses. It represents a sophisticated blend of art and science designed to maintain and enhance your company's financial health, ensuring it can support and prioritize ambitious scaling efforts and, most importantly, help you glance around the corner, so to speak, to see what's ahead.

Your cash flow projection tool, which can be managed by a basic bookkeeper, CFO, or even yourself (depending on the size and complexity of your business), should include a process that involves rigorous budgeting of planned expenses (outflows), forecasting of revenues (inflows) with a high degree of confidence, and understanding the timing intricacies between these elements. This understanding helps determine your working capital needs (otherwise known as the "float")—the necessary cash required to operate the business. While working capital needs and net working capital are not identical, having a grasp on both is beneficial for comprehensive cash management.

Your cash projection tool should offer a detailed view of your finances for the upcoming four to 12 weeks, with a monthly projection extending over the 12 months, updated on a rolling weekly basis. This tool should serve as your roadmap, showing where funds are being allocated and identifying any potential shortfalls. This rhythm of money coming in and out determines the company's liquidity, affecting its ability to respond to unexpected challenges or capitalize on sudden opportunities.

By proactively forecasting future expenses and revenue, you gain a strategic advantage, allowing you to prepare for upcoming financial conditions more effectively. Like any significant key metric, frequent check-ins on cash are essential. Daily or weekly reviews of financial metrics related to your cash flows are highly recommended and can identify areas of risk before they become catastrophic. These timely assessments allow you to make swift, informed decisions, helping ensure steady financial navigation, even during business volatility, uncertainty, or tough economic climates.

Access our Cash Flow Compass tool at ReadyForScaling.com/resources.

Mastering the Cash Conversion Cycle

For simplicity, cash conversion cycle (or CCC) measures the time it takes for each dollar invested in inventory (if you're a product company) or labor (if you're a service company) to flow back into your company in the form of cash from sales. It's a vital indicator of a company's operational efficiency and liquidity. With that in mind, let's explore a somewhat counterintuitive yet pivotal concept in funding growth from within: the negative cash conversion cycle.

A negative cash conversion cycle is often a foreign concept to most business owners, yet its power cannot be understated. It occurs when a business manages to receive payments from customers *before* it is required to pay its suppliers, hence creating a cash inflow prior to the correlated outflow covering expenses related to that particular sale. This brilliant yet elusive financial strategy reduces reliance on external funding by leveraging internal operating income to fuel growth. Why this approach to financing growth is so commonly overlooked baffles me, but it's one of the first places we explore whenever engaging with a new client.

Perhaps it's because achieving a negative CCC involves a sophisticated approach encompassing seven key levers of cash flow—which we will detail shortly—and a nuanced approach to supplier negotiations, hastening customer payments, and adopting just-in-time inventory management. In other words, it takes work and a detailed roadmap, but the rewards can be wildly beneficial to your company. Let's just say the impact of mastering the cash conversion cycle is profound, potentially allowing your business to avoid substantial debt or equity financing by instead using internally generated cash flow. Make no mistake, even if your company can't fully reverse your

CCC, the process will still yield significant benefits. Overall, the effort to improve your CCC will strengthen your company's financial health and strategic position.

Let's look at a first-hand case study of exemplary cash management in action...

A Mini-Case in Achieving Superior Negative Cash Conversion

Here's how our company, QuickBox, was able to pull this off and build a negative cash conversion cycle so strong that it was able to finance our scale to over $100 million without ever putting any money into the company, taking on a penny of debt, or giving up precious equity.

The process began with a thorough review of our value chain, service cycle, and cash flow implications—both incoming and outgoing. We assumed basic unit economics of sales (order fulfillment in this instance) and set about optimizing each step until we reached a negative cash conversion.

Next, we looked at how we organized credit terms with our clients: we arranged for payments (inflow) on our order fulfillment services within five to seven days, based on weekly invoicing. Our primary expenditure (outflow), labor, was scheduled for payment every two weeks. Further cash flow efficiencies were gained by consolidating client postage costs into a single account, which we negotiated with our carrier. We repackaged and sold postage back to our clients at a discount, billing in the same manner as our other services. However, we also negotiated net 30 terms with cur postage carrier, allowing us to turn a small profit and substantial timing on our cash surplus.

Our final and most critical element was our approach to product inventory. This is where our strategy differed from other order fulfillment centers. We supplied products like nutritional supplements and skincare items on-demand, using a just-in-time model to meet client needs. Simultaneously, we negotiated consignment terms with our private label manufacturers, who only billed us for inventory as it was sold (outflow) on net 15 credit terms. Our clients were billed under the same terms for products (inflow) as they were for our other services—net 7, enhancing our cash surplus even more.

This approach wasn't merely about savvy financial calculations. It was critical to cultivate relationships and collaborate with partners to buy into a mutually beneficial vision that promised mutual benefits. The result was an extraordinarily effective negative cash conversion cycle, generating a surplus of cash that financed our periods of explosive growth, benefiting all stakeholders involved—our clients, our partners, and our business.

By using this cash flow arrangement while running QuickBox, we were essentially able to produce a staggering $5.8 million in surplus (available) cash flow. Here's how the CCC calculation worked out...

Assuming an annual revenue of $100 million, this translates to approximately $274,000 in daily income earnings. For the sake of this illustration, let's assume that every day involves fulfilling 20,000 orders. While not every order might include products sold to clients, simplifying this scenario to include them in each order helps clarify the financial dynamics we're discussing. This setup provides a practical framework for understanding the scale of operations and the financial throughput necessary to support such a business model.

As such, let's review the inflows and outflows and show you the daily and cumulative impact on cash surplus over the payment cycles:

Daily Inflows

Order Ful-fillment:	$2.50 per order x 20,000 orders	$50,000 per day	Received in 7 days
Postage:	$5.00 per order x 20,000 orders	$100,000 per day	Received in 7 days
Products:	$7.00 per order x 20,000 orders	$140,000 per day	Received in 7 days

Daily Outflows

Labor (60% of order fulfillment):	$2.50 x 60% = $1.50 per order / $1.50 x 20,000 orders	$30,000 per day	Paid every two weeks (14 days)
Postage:	$5.00 per order x 20,000 orders	$100,000 per day	Payment due in 30 days
Products:	- $3.50 per product x 2 products per order = $7.00 per order / $7.00 x 20,000 orders - $7.00 x 20,000 orders = $140,000 per day	$140,000 per day	Payment due in 15 days

Cash Flow Timing

Inflows:	$290,000 per day	All received in 7 days
Outflows:	- Labor = $30,000 per day, due in 14 days.	Staggered payments: Due in 14 days

	- Postage = $100,000 per day, due in 30 days. - Products = S140,000 per day, due in 15 days.	Due in 30 days Due in 15 days

Calculation of Cash Surplus

		Daily Surplus
Days 1 – 6:	No outflows, only inflows	$290,000
Days 7 – 13:	Labor outflow begins from Day 14	$290,000
Day 14:	Labor pay-ment starts	$290,000 - $30,000 = $260,000
Day 15:	Product pay-ment starts	$290,000 - $30,000 - $140,000 = $120,000
Days 16 – 29:	Continue as Day 15	$120,000
Day 30:	Postage pay-ment starts	$290,000 - $30,000 - $140,000 - $100,000 = $20,000

Cumulative Cash Surplus

Days 1 – 14:	Accumulated surplus before labor payout starts.	Total = 14 days x $290,000 = $4,060,000
Days 15 – 29:	Accumulated surplus before the product and postage payouts start.	Additional total from Day 15 to Day 29 = 15 days x $120,000 = $1,800,000
Day 30 and onward:	Reduced surplus due to all payments being active.	Daily surplus of **$20,000** (This continues daily until inflow/outflow schedule resets or changes.)
Total Surplus		**$5,880,000**

End Result of The Negative Cash Conversion Cycle Analysis

This calculation illustrates how a company like QuickBox could maintain a significant cash surplus daily until all payments are active. As a result, the cash on hand before significant outflows (up to Day 14) highlights the strength of the negative CCC, allowing the business to use internal funds effectively without the immediate need for external financing.

While this specific creative approach might differ for your company, optimizing each inflow and outflow demonstrates effective cash flow management to sustain operations and support even the most rapid growth.

Fine-Tuning Your Cash Flow with the 7 Levers Cash Navigator

When it comes to managing cash flow and optimizing your cash conversion cycle, it's about strategically manipulating certain levers to not only maintain financial health but also support and even internally fund growth. Here, we introduce our proprietary tool called "The 7 Levers Cash Navigator," which we originally designed to guide our consulting clients through the critical financial decisions that shape their cash conversion cycle. Each lever is designed to be interactive, providing a clear understanding of how varying actions impact your financial stability.

Access the 7 Levers Cash Navigator Tool at ReadyForScaling.com/resources.

Let's explore the 7 Levers and their roles in optimizing cash flow:

1. **Pricing:**
Adjusting the pricing of your products or services is crucial for optimizing revenue. Effective pricing strategies should reflect the perceived value to the customer and market demand. Properly set prices enhance cash inflow, whereas mispricing can lead to reduced profits or even customer churn. (The fastest way to improve cash flow is to increase prices!)

2. **Volume:**

Sales volume directly influences cash flow; increasing volume (order throughput) or service velocity typically enhances overall cash inflow. However, it's essential to balance this with production capacity and market demand to prevent issues like excess inventory or strained labor.

3. **Cost of Goods Sold (COGS):**

Managing the direct costs associated with producing your goods or services is pivotal. By controlling these costs, you can enhance your gross margin. While reducing COGS and operating expenses is beneficial for cash flow, care must be taken not to compromise the quality of your products or operational service capabilities.

4. **Accounts Receivable:**

Efficient management of accounts receivable is key to accelerating cash inflow. Strategies like shortening payment terms or improving the collection processes can significantly speed up cash turnover, thereby improving liquidity and cash availability.

5. **Inventory Management:**

Optimizing inventory levels strikes a balance between meeting customer demand and minimizing holding costs. Remember, every excess product held in inventory is a dollar equivalent less in cash available. The silent killer here is product inventory that goes obsolete. Effective inventory management ensures you avoid tying up excessive cash in stock while preventing stock-outs that could lead to lost sales.

6. Accounts Payable:

Careful management of accounts payable helps control cash outflows. By negotiating and managing the timing and terms of payments to suppliers and vendors, you can conserve cash, but it's important to maintain healthy supplier relationships and adhere to favorable credit terms.

7. Overhead Expenses (OpEx):

Controlling overhead expenses is essential for maintaining healthy cash flow. Overhead expenses include fixed costs such as rent, utilities, salaries, and technology. By managing these costs effectively, businesses can reduce unnecessary expenditures and increase available cash. Effective overhead management ensures that more revenue contributes directly to profit and cash reserves, strengthening the company's financial stability.

Though it's not included in traditional operational expenses of your business, taking advantage of debt financing options can support your business's growth. That said, it's far too easy to drown in debt, tying up too much cash in interest payments. Paying attention to this area involves managing repayment obligations and avoiding excessive interest expenses, which can put a drain on cash flow. This lever should be looked at separately—and used judiciously—to maintain a balance between leveraging growth opportunities and sustaining financial health.

Access our 7 Levers Cash Navigator at ReadyForScaling.com/resources.

The beauty of the 7 Levers tool is that it allows you to simulate various scenarios to see the potential impacts on your cash flow immediately, using a single lever or multiple levers. This interactivity makes it an invaluable resource for planning, prioritizing, and decision-making surrounding your cash. By optimizing these levers, you can enhance your financial foresight, plan how to improve cash flow, and drive sustainable growth.

Assessing Your "Growth Capital" Requirements

Before setting out on the journey of scaling your business, there is a fundamental question we pose to every client: *"If I handed you $1 million today, how would you spend it on your company, and what return would you expect it to generate for your company?"*

Often, this question is met with a blank stare. Occasionally, a well-prepared entrepreneur, having previously pondered this scenario, might offer a ready answer. This question isn't just theoretical—it's a crucial part of preparing for growth and, if necessary (whether it's more or less money), seeking investment.

Understanding the capital required to support your business's growth is essential. Moreover, it's vital to have a clear plan for how this money will be used and the expected revenue growth this "capital requirement" will generate. As discussed earlier, financing for scaling can come from internal sources, such as operating income, or, depending on the requirements, from external capital sources. Or, a well-crafted combination of both sources.

The process of determining your business's growth capital requirements traditionally involves developing a financial forecast model that defines the capital needed to support projected growth. While constructing this model is typically complex and time-consuming, for the sake of clarity and progress, we've simplified the approach to make it understandable and actionable. This calculated figure, which we call the "growth capital requirement," must be rigorously tested. It will serve as a critical metric, scrutinized against the backdrop of our anticipated business performance.

The exercise of calculating your growth capital requirement isn't just about coming up with a number—it's about envisioning and planning your company's future. It forces you to think strategically about resource allocation and to critically evaluate the potential return on every dollar invested. This foresight and strategic planning are indispensable as you prepare to scale your business, ensuring every investment made is geared toward sustainable growth and increased profitability.

Here's an example of how we computed this for an existing client…

Calculating the Capital Growth Requirement—A Mini-Case Study on a Pet Supplements Co

Using a client, Holistapet, a pet supplement company, here is precisely how we calculated their growth capital requirements to support scaling their brand (where the numbers have been changed for confidentiality purposes). Holistatpet is a direct-to-consumer consumer packaged goods company anticipating 50 percent year-over-year growth, outsourced its manufacturing of products, relied on a variable model of warehousing and order fulfillment, and was well aware of its marketing metrics—the three most important being (i) customer acquisition cost (CAC), (ii) average order value (AOV), and (iii) expected frequency of purchases (which equates to customer lifetime value, or CLV). On that basis, we constructed a financial model with toggleable inputs, which allows for dynamic scenario planning and better decision-making. Here's how we set up such a model:

Simplified Capital Requirements Model
(normally modeled within a comprehensive worksheet)

Step 1: Revenue Projection

Metric	Value	Formula
Current Annual Revenue	$1,000,000	Historical Data

Growth Target	50%	Strategic Target
Projected Annual Revenue	$1,500,000	Current Annual Revenue * (1 + Growth Target)

Step 2: Incremental Costs

Metric	Value	Formula
COGS as % of Sales	40%	Historical Data
Projected COGS	$600,000	Projected Annual Revenue * COGS %
Customer Acquisition Cost (CAC)	$20	Historical Data
Average Order Value (AOV)	$100	Historical Data
Marketing Spend Needed	$100,000	(Annual Revenue Increase / AOV) * CAC

Step 3: Working Capital

Metric	Value	Formula
Additional Inventory Needed	$200,000	(Projected Rev – Current Rev) * COGS %
Accounts Receivable Increase	$4.11	Projected Annual Revenue increase * (AR Period *(=3 days, common for DTC)* / 365 Days)

Step 4: Operational Costs

Metric	Value	Formula
Variable Costs	$50,000	Rev Increase * historical % of sales
Fixed Costs	$50,000	Based on forecasted expenses required to support growth

Step 5: Calculation of Total Capital Requirements

Metric	Value	Formula
Total Operational Costs	$100,000	Increase in Fixed + Variable Costs
Increase in Working Capital	$200,004	Additional Inventory + AR Increase
Total Capital Requirement Increase to Support Growth	$550,004	Total Variable Costs + Marketing Spend + Increase in Working Capital

When completed, this "working projection model" should allow you to simulate different scenarios and immediately see the financial impacts, enabling strategic decisions about how much is needed to finance your growth (e.g., internal cash flow vs. external funding sources).

By having these inputs toggleable, you can more easily adjust assumptions and see how sensitive your capital requirements are to different operational and market conditions.

The example above requires a company to produce an additional ~$550,000 in working capital to produce an additional $500,000 in revenue—highlighting how expensive growth can be and the significant capital requirements associated with scaling a business. A key caveat to this simplified model is that it assumes 100 percent of the growth comes from acquiring new customers, without accounting for increased purchase frequency or a higher number of returning customers. Consequently, this model errs on the side of presenting the most expensive case scenario.

Planning for the worst-case scenario, or at least a more pragmatic scenario, has several benefits. It ensures that a business is financially prepared for the highest potential costs, reducing the risk of underfunding its growth. This conservative approach also provides a buffer for unforeseen expenses and challenges, enhancing the company's financial resilience. By anticipating and planning for the maximum growth capital requirements, you can secure sufficient funding (whether external or internal), avoid cash flow issues, and maintain operational stability during periods of rapid growth.

The Eternal Dilemma: Seeking External Funding

Internal funding is our preferred method of financing when scaling a business, akin to fueling growth from within. That being said, there are times in a company's expansion when external funding becomes a necessary accelerant—like throwing gasoline onto a fire fueled with oxygen, where a restriction of cash can suffocate the most explosive growth. Before exploring this avenue, however, it's essential to critically assess the real need for such funds.

It's vital when exploring various funding options to understand their implications and choose the most suitable one for your business. While we won't dive into each funding type here (you can find a detailed list with their pros and cons on our website at ReadyForScaling.com), remember that choosing between debt and equity is a crucial and, sometimes, life-altering decision. Debt has to be repaid, often with interest, and opting for equity involves trading a portion of your future value for immediate capital. It's wise to guard your equity fiercely and make such decisions based on expert advice (like a qualified attorney), considering the availability of funding options, the valuation of your enterprise, the specifics of the deal, and the qualities of the capital partner.

As an entrepreneur, deciding to take on external funding is not just a business decision but a personal one, as your company is often seen as your "baby." So, it *must* be approached with great care. Furthermore, if opting for debt, you should ensure that you have a robust financial plan showing you can service this debt comfortably, ideally maintaining a coverage ratio of at least three to five times EBITDA (earnings before interest, taxes, and depreciation).

I learned the critical importance of this the hard way. During a particularly challenging phase of one of my prior businesses, I faced the daunting reality of my banker calling in our $2.5-million line of credit, which we were desperately struggling to service. That meeting ranks as one of the worst days of my life, a moment when I saw both my business and my personal life teetering on the edge. Yet, it was also a turning point.

With an incredibly dedicated and loyal team behind me, we rallied together. I was transparent about our dire situation and invited those on our executive team who felt unable to commit to the recovery effort to leave gracefully; only one did. Together, we navigated through the crisis, repaid every penny of debt, and simultaneously launched a groundbreaking new product that paved the way for our company's recovery.

Our efforts didn't just save the company; they propelled us to new heights, culminating in taking the company public (found today on NASDAQ under the symbol "FTLF") and raising nearly $10 million in growth equity.

This experience underscored two critical lessons: as famously attributed to Winston Churchill, *"Never let a good crisis go to waste."* Perhaps more importantly, always stay keenly attuned to your financial metrics and heed the warnings they afford you. My oversight, hubris, and complacency nearly cost us everything, teaching me the invaluable lessons of humility, trust in my team, and hyper-vigilant financial oversight.

Investing Cash Intelligently in the Scaling Journey

Every scaling journey requires an investment of capital—whether it's your own internally generated income or an outside source of capital investment. Regardless, the magic lies in knowing precisely when to invest it, where to allocate it, and what returns to expect in terms of revenue and profit growth. Cash is the crucial link that bridges this chasm and connects your current position to your future aspirations.

Managing cash flow might seem complex, but it doesn't have to be overwhelming or daunting. Armed with the right tools and frameworks, even those without a financial background can confidently steer through the complexities of business finance. Tools such as the Cash Flow Planner, Growth Capital Requirement calculator, and The 7 Levers Cash Navigator are designed to help you streamline this process, enabling smarter, more informed financial decisions.

As we close this chapter, cash appears last within our principles-centered framework, not because it is the least important but because it is the capstone. It's the final essential piece that supports all other aspects of a scaling venture. It ensures that every other element—from operational efficiency to market expansion—is adequately funded and poised for success. Yet, simultaneously, every prior step in the process ensures the cash availability is being put to its best, most impactful use. By understanding and managing your cash flow effectively, you set the stage for sustainable growth and long-term profitability.

Now, with the five essential pillars of our scaling framework clearly defined and in mind, it's time to turn our attention to a crucial prerequisite that, although sometimes too easily overlooked or shrugged off, deserves our focused attention before we embark on our scaling journey. This essential element is ensuring a solid product-market fit...

PART THREE:

Scaling Sustainably

Chapter 10

Product-Market Fit—The Gateway to Scaling Your Business

Before you accelerate the growth of your business, it's vital to confirm that your product or service not only meets a genuine market need but does so in a way that outshines competitors.

This prerequisite criterion, which was brought up earlier, is worth repeating: a strong product-market fit is the foundation upon which successful scaling is built. Not having product-market fit while trying to scale would be akin to spinning your wheels faster and faster but not going anywhere. Without it, efforts to scale will be extremely inefficient, wasting valuable resources—time, money, effort, opportunity—and if not fixed or pivoted soon enough, ultimately leading to the unwelcome death of the venture itself.

By thoroughly validating your product or service's appeal and its market demand, you position your business for effective scaling, equipped with the confidence that your offerings will attract and retain customers. This validation acts as a critical checkpoint, ensuring all subsequent investments in scaling are both justified and likely to produce significant returns. Therefore, although it was presented earlier as a prerequisite to scaling, we felt it was essential to dedicate an entire chapter to discuss it more in-depth. This will help you ensure you get (or have gotten) this critical factor right *before* we march along on our scaling journey.

(Sidenote: to keep things more streamlined, when we say "product" in the context of this chapter, it can be used interchangeably with "service," depending on your business model.)

This chapter will not only clarify the concept of product-market fit but will also equip you with robust frameworks and real-world examples to measure and achieve product-market fit effectively. In addition, we're going to dive deeper into The Diamond Strategic Positioning Grid, a critical tool we'll explore in detail that helps pinpoint your product's exact position in the market, ensuring your scaling efforts are built on the cornerstone of market demand and competitive positioning.

By the end of this chapter, you'll not only understand what product-market fit is but also how to assess it dynamically as your market and product evolve.

Timing: The Crucial Element of Product-Market Validation

Consider this enlightening observation by Bill Gross from Palo Alto Labs: after empirically studying the thousands of startup ventures he's worked with, he found the most significant determinant of startup success isn't the idea, the team, the business model, or even the funding—*it's timing*, contributing to success 42 percent of the time. This is because timing ensures a product hits the market at just the right moment, neither too early nor too late, but right when the tsunami of market acceptance and subsequent demand is building. A product launched too soon might meet market resistance due to a lack of readiness or understanding, while a late entry might very well struggle in an overcrowded market filled with competitors.

Drawing from my vault of product launch experiences, in 2007, I partnered with Joel Appel, a legendary figure in the business world known for his key role in the success of brands like OxyClean and Orange Glo, which were later sold to Church & Dwight. We partnered to commercialize two innovative products I had created. The first was Voots, a fruit and vegetable chewable tart for kids made with all-natural ingredients. The second, PreMira, was a collagen peptide ready-to-drink protein supplement intended for health and beauty improvements in women.

Before spending any money on a product launch, Joel firmly believed that the real test of a product's potential was a consumer's willingness to part ways with their hard-earned cash for it. This belief led us to a unique method of initial validation: setting up a kiosk in a local shopping mall to sell our products directly to consumers. This direct interaction provided invaluable insights into consumer behavior, preferences, frequently asked questions and objections, various price points, and the product's market readiness.

Market Validation: The Tale of Two Products

Our first product, Voots, was an instant hit. After kids sampled the chews and showed visible approval, their parents were quick to inquire about the price, leading to a sell-out scenario. In fact, we had to cancel the second day of kiosk rental since we had run out of stock. This immediate and overwhelming acceptance indicated perfect market timing and product validation for a children's nutritional supplement.

Conversely, our experience with PreMira was humbling. Despite our best efforts at the same mall on a different weekend, we did not sell a single unit. Every interaction, regardless of the price point or sales pitch, ended in rejection. The market simply wasn't ready for collagen supplements. The prevailing perception was that collagen was for external (hands and face) use only, not ingestion (as a drink). This resistance highlighted a significant market education gap that, at the time, would be too costly to bridge.

Interestingly, if you visit stores like Whole Foods or Sprouts today, you'll find collagen peptide supplements prominently displayed everywhere you turn, suggesting the market has since evolved to embrace the concept of "beauty from within." This shift underscores how critical timing is: our idea was sound, but in 2007, the market was not prepared.

Voots, on the other hand, went on to earn retail placement in stores like Costco, Target, Walmart, Kroger, and several thousands of additional points of sale. It ended up becoming a huge success by consumer-packaged goods distribution standards, and we eventually sold it to Pharmavite, America's largest vitamin manufacturer and reseller.

These experiences underscore the profound impact of timing on product-market success. While Voots aligned perfectly with market readiness, PreMira's introduction was premature. The lesson here is clear: understanding and predicting market trends are as critical as the product itself. No amount of funding or marketing can compensate for a misaligned launch time. This alignment, more often than not, determines their ultimate success or failure.

In his popular TedTalk, Bill Gross shared his empirical findings, those factors that ultimately determine a startup's success, in order of importance:

- Timing (42%)
- Team/Execution (32%)
- Idea (28%)
- Business Model (24%)
- Funding (14%)

Our Three Techniques for Assessing Product-Market Fit

TECHNIQUE 1) Understanding Market Scalability Potential: TAM, SAM, & SOM

When plotting the course for a product's journey, after assessing category timing, we find three notable navigational metrics helpful to understand before scaling: the Total Addressable Market (TAM), Serviceable Addressable Market (SAM), and Serviceable Obtainable Market (SOM). These metrics aren't just lofty numbers. They are the bedrock of strategic decision-making. TAM helps you understand the full potential of the market—how big your pie could theoretically be if you convinced 100 percent of every potential customer to buy your product. SAM, on the other hand, narrows down this perspective to the portion of the market you can actually service; where SOM aims to pinpoint the *actual* share or market you *project* to capture, given your current product category, business model, capabilities, and geographic reach.

Calculating these isn't about pulling numbers out of thin air but involves a careful analysis of market data, consumer trends, and competitive landscapes. Knowing these figures helps you gauge whether the ocean you're planning to fish in is vast and abundant or just a small pond. More simply put, understanding the TAM, SAM, and SOM sets the stage for answering a critical question: *Is there enough market to scale into effectively?* These metrics define the possible scalability or, said another way, your potential rewards of getting product-market fit right.

Mini Case Study: HoochBooch's Big Pivot

Consider the example of the female-founded HoochBooch, whose brilliant CEO I've mentored—a daring brand that ventured into the beverage world of "hard kombucha." While the broader alcohol market is a billion-dollar playground, HoochBooch targeted the considerably smaller niche of alcoholic kombucha—a market still in its infancy and resisting consumer expansion. Soon after launch, the company found itself faced with significant challenges, not only due to the limited size of the serviceable market but also because kombucha itself requires a developed palette and certain health-oriented consumer education. Despite the general allure of alcoholic drinks, HoochBooch consistently struggled to broaden its appeal beyond the niche audience accustomed to kombucha's unique taste.

In working with the founder, Anna, I was convinced the product was competing in a "fringe niche," considering the size and complexity of its audience and limited customer base. And, when evaluating the upside potential, it was evident that the return on the company's time and effort wasn't sufficient to pursue and, based on the math, surely wouldn't materialize an adequate return on any invested capital.

The lesson here is stark: even with a great product that fits within a broader category with immense potential, understanding the nuances of your serviceable market is critical. It wasn't just about selling an alcoholic beverage. It was about selling a type of alcoholic beverage to a market segment that was both unfamiliar and underdeveloped.

Fortunately, Anna recognized the consumer adoption challenges of her initial market and shifted her focus to a burgeoning segment— functional beverages. Leveraging her extensive background in hospitality and the insights gained from her original beverage launch, Anna introduced a groundbreaking new product, Corpse Reviver.

This functional beverage—with a quirky name, creative packaging design, and refreshing taste—quickly captured the attention of the industry and consumers alike, earning the prestigious NEXTY award for innovation in beverages at the Natural Products Expo.

Following this accolade, Corpse Reviver soared in popularity, becoming a staple in restaurants, natural food stores, and bars, particularly as a sought-after mocktail by the poolside.

TECHNIQUE 2) Introducing the Diamond Strategic Positioning Grid

Whether it's pre- or post-launch of your product, embarking on the quest for product-market fit can often feel like trying to find a diamond in the rough. Fittingly, that's where our exclusive Diamond Strategic Positioning Grid comes into play. While we would normally use this tool during the strategic planning phase, it doesn't promise the elusive guarantee of a perfect market fit, it serves as a valuable *guide* for navigating the complex landscape of market positioning with an eye toward sustainable competitive advantage.

The Diamond Strategic Positioning Grid is a tool I put together during my time teaching strategy at the University of Denver. It was created to help assess where a product stands in the competitive arena, providing a clearer understanding of its current positioning and even helps guide its strategic aspirations.

It's structured with two key axes: **differentiation** and **protectability**. On the left-hand side, you evaluate differentiation—does your product wedge out the market because of its low-cost pricing strategy, or does it outshine due to technological innovation? Moving to the right-hand side, you consider protectability—does your product have robust legal defenses like a patent, or does it face the risk of becoming commoditized?

Placement on the grid, and the intersection of both axes where your product fits, determines its likelihood for a superior competitive advantage in the market—thereby improving its opportunity for sustainable product-market fit.

Access The Diamond Strategic Positioning Grid Tool at ReadyForScaling.com/resources.

Application of the Diamond Strategic Positioning Grid (more detailed examples of how to use it can be found on ReadyForScaling.com)

Using the Diamond Strategic Positioning Grid involves a systematic approach to analyzing and positioning your product or service in the marketplace. Here's a summary step-by-step guide to navigating this strategic tool:

Step 1. Identify Your Differentiation

Start by pinpointing what makes your product unique. Is it cost-effective enough to undercut competitors, or does it offer a novel functionality others can't replicate? Place your product on the left side of the grid based on its primary competitive edge.

Step 2. Assess Your Protectability

Next, evaluate how well your product can be shielded from competitors. Are there patents or trade secrets that secure its uniqueness, or is it vulnerable to imitation? This assessment goes on the right side of the grid.

Step 3. Analyze Market Position

With your product's placement on both axes, analyze its overall market position—its intersecting points from each axis. A product positioned toward both high differentiation and high protectability is at the top of the "diamond zone"—optimal for sustainability and competitive advantage.

Step 4. Strategic Decision-Making

Use the insights gained from the Diamond Strategic Positioning Grid to make informed strategic decisions. If your product is highly differentiated but low on protectability, consider ways to enhance its defenses. Conversely, if it's highly protectable but lacks differentiation, focus on adding or highlighting unique features or benefits.

By following these steps in assessing product-market fit potential, the Diamond Strategic Positioning Grid helps you crystalize your product's market position, guiding you toward strategic choices that enhance its chances of a sustainable product-market fit success in a competitive landscape.

Make no mistake, success can be achieved from any point on the Diamond Strategic Positioning Grid. However, the design of the tool suggests that the higher you position your product or service toward the top, the greater likelihood of achieving product success, or even market dominance, with potentially less competitive resistance. To get the most out of the tool, the primary objective is to plot where you currently stand based on your existing capabilities, while also envisioning (and plotting) where you aim to be in the future. This forward-thinking approach helps craft a strategic path beyond product-market fit and toward a more sustainable competitive advantage by advancing closer to the top of the Diamond Strategic Positioning Grid.

TECHNIQUE 3) Measuring the "Stickiness" of Product-Market Fit

Measuring product-market fit isn't quite as straightforward as it may seem—it involves a blend of both art and science. In this area, we're looking for the product's stickiness found with end consumers. Once the product has been launched, we need to speedily navigate through various quantitative and qualitative metrics that together signal whether a product and its market are indeed finding a fit. These metrics can range from user engagement rates to customer satisfaction surveys, each providing a piece of the larger puzzle. There are three primary measurements to assess in evaluating whether you've found, or at least are on the right track, to product-market fit:

A. Customer Feedback and Reviews

The voice of the customer is your North Star. Collecting and analyzing customer feedback isn't just about tallying up the smiles and frowns. It's about diving deep into the psyche of your users—what delights them, what frustrates them, and what would make them recommend your product to their best friend or mother-in-law. Surveys, Net Promoter Scores (NPS), and online reviews (from Google, Yotpo, TrustPilot, or wherever you can collate them) can be easily deployed and serve as your diagnosis here, uncovering the signals to satisfaction and areas needing improvement. Remember, every piece of feedback should be treated like a golden ticket to refining your product and, ultimately, finding a better fit in the market.

B. Engagement and Usage Statistics

Engagement metrics are the silent whispers of your customers, telling you how often and how deeply they interact with your product. Do they visit your website and bounce, or do they linger and eventually buy something? Do they use your app once and forget about it, or do they come back like they can't get enough of it? Analyzing these patterns through marketing metrics like frequency of purchase, growth in net subscribers, and lifetime value (over at least a 180-day period) helps you understand not just if people like your product but if they find it indispensable and truly love it.

C. Sales Growth Metrics

Lastly, the proof is often in the pudding—or, in this case, in the sales data. Sales growth metrics are your scoreboard. They tell you if more people are buying what you're selling. Are sales steady, growing month over month, or spiking in any particular consumer segment, geographic area, or retail chain? Is there a correlation between any recent marketing campaigns or product augmentations? This data doesn't just confirm product-market fit. It also shows the trajectory of your growth—whether you're scaling a steep cliff, riding a gentle slope, or on a slow descent.

Each area of measurement is designed to provide a deeper understanding of the essential methods to measure product-market fit. Understanding these metrics will help you not just guess but know whether you're on the right track or whether you've hit paydirt with product-market fit.

Let's explore these examples in greater detail, with a mini-case study from one of my prior product launches that failed to find product-market fit but eventually became a household name...

Mini Case Study: The Fast-Acting, Long-Lasting Energy Product Desperately Seeking Its Market

In 2005, while at the helm of my nutritional supplement company, we took an exciting turn when we decided to tackle the common pitfalls of the traditional energy market. We launched a groundbreaking nutritional supplement product named Energize, engineered to sidestep the notorious spikes and crashes associated with caffeine and the then wildly popular "energy shot" category. Instead, this energy pill was designed to deliver a smooth, sustained energy boost lasting up to eight hours, thanks to a sophisticated manufacturing process. Our bold claims were not just marketing hype. They were backed by multiple randomized, double-blind, placebo-controlled clinical studies—the gold standard of scientific research.

When we introduced the product to the market, the initial reception was lukewarm at best. At first, our marketing efforts were geared toward fitness enthusiasts and gym-goers, whom we believed would be the primary beneficiaries of our sustained energy solution. However, the sales did not meet our expectations, prompting us to probe deeper into our customer base.

Through detailed surveys and interactions with end-users, we uncovered a surprising trend. The typical users of our product were not the fitness buffs we had originally envisioned. Instead, it found favor among an entirely different demographic—truck drivers needing to stay alert, nurses working long shifts, and stay-at-home parents juggling busy schedules. These individuals sought a reliable energy boost without the volume of traditional energy drinks or the intense rush from energy shots. They also did not want to spend all their money on the daily pick-me-up allure of Starbucks.

Armed with these insights, we quickly pivoted. We overhauled our packaging (moving from dark blue to bright yellow) to appeal to this broader audience and strategically modified our pricing strategy (moving our price point below $15) to offer greater value yet minimize retail channel conflict.

Then, we strategically repositioned our product in the market. We launched targeted advertising campaigns on radio stations, specifically during segments popular with morning and afternoon commuters.

Doing this opened up opportunities for us to pursue strategic retail partnerships, placing our product on the shelves of Walmart, Walgreens, CVS, and other outlets frequented by our newly identified customer base. This strategic pivot paid off spectacularly. Nearly two decades later, Energize not only remains a top-selling product in the company's portfolio, but it has also enjoyed a long-standing presence in major retail outlets—spanning almost 20 years on the shelf at Walmart and selling over one billion servings since its launch.

This mini case study illustrates the profound impact of responsive market repositioning and the importance of listening to customer feedback to find product-market fit. By stepping back to analyze and act on the insights gathered from actual product use, we were able to transform a modest start into a resounding market success. Energize's journey from a fitness supplement to an everyday essential product highlights the critical role of adaptability in unlocking a product's full scalable potential in the market.

As we conclude this chapter, I'm unsure when I came across this saying or who said it, but it always stuck with me: "*To allure is an art; to retain is mastery*." As we march forward in our quest to amplify your company's scale, let's keep in mind that positioning your product to create and sustain a competitive advantage against your competitors—while maintaining a consistent and predictable customer acquisition strategy—is the ultimate goal to finding and keeping product-market fit.

In other words: charm your customers, cherish them, retain them, and always treat them like everyone's watching—because in the transparent world of today's business, they most certainly are.

Now, before we start putting our learnings into action, we need to talk about an important discipline that definingly separates the companies that scale from those that fail: the discipline of execution...

Chapter 11

The Discipline of Execution—The Final Element to Scaling Success

Imagine walking into an office where the buzz of frantic activity is barely palpable. People huddled around their laptops and phones, scurrying to read the latest *urgent* email sent from their CEO—a scene of sheer entrepreneurial bewilderment and terror. Now, also imagine, amidst this chaos, the founder of this company sitting, head turned down in hands, pondering, "I can't believe we're closing the doors and shutting down our business… Where did we go wrong?"

Welcome to a day in the life of a scaling enterprise that missed the memo on discipline:

The discipline of execution.

The power of execution is so pivotal that entire books have been devoted to it, highlighting its role as a fundamental determinant of a company's success. As we shift your business into scaling mode, the ability to execute with precision and efficiency becomes increasingly significant.

Discipline truly shines in the execution phase. It's one thing to have a plan; it's another to execute it effectively. Discipline ensures that plans don't just stay on paper. Instead, they translate into ownership, actions, and results.

Disciplined execution involves setting clear goals, assigning responsibilities, monitoring progress, and making necessary adjustments. It's like a well-oiled machine—every part works in sync to achieve the desired outcome. Discipline isn't glamorous. Even though there are plenty of books written about the subject; it's rarely even talked about inside the entrepreneurial ecosystem. But make no mistake, the discipline of execution is *truly* what differentiates the winners from the rest. And from our experience, it can become a cultural fixture that creates a competitive advantage that separates your company even further from competitors.

The Essence of Discipline in Scaling

Discipline in business isn't about maintaining stern faces and adhering to rigid rules. It's about establishing a good rhythm—a consistent cadence to which every component of the organization syncs, moving in unison toward a shared vision. Picture it as a well-orchestrated symphony—each instrument plays its part, precisely and on time, culminating in a harmonious output.

This disciplined approach ensures that, regardless of the challenges encountered, the business consistently *gets sh*t done* and achieves its day-to-day tasks, completes its outstanding projects, culminating in the realization of longer-term objectives. It's about an embedded sense of urgency with a bias toward action, prioritizing progress over perfection, and creating a culture where the pursuit of improvement is valued more than faultless execution.

Once this mindset takes hold, a culture of disciplined execution becomes voracious and nearly unstoppable, propelling the business toward scalable and sustainable growth.

In contrast, an undisciplined organization often resembles a band where every musician plays a different tune. The result? Discordance. For instance, consider Company Y (a real-life example with a fictional name for confidentiality purposes). They had brilliant ideas, enthusiastic teams, and a thriving business, but the team lacked a disciplined approach to accountability and execution. It was quite normal to skip, push, or cancel meetings entirely. They ran the business absent of any formal operating management system. There was an allergy to accountability, where excuses and finger-pointing were the norm. The outcome was a series of missed deadlines, unhappy customers, and a talented but directionless workforce.

The Framework of Discipline

The discipline of execution is about making things happen—efficiently and consistently. It's about converting strategic plans into tangible outcomes.

In scaling, this means not just chasing new opportunities but, more importantly, scaling off the existing commitments and delivering with excellence.

Effective execution hinges on two key elements: *clarity* and *accountability*. Everyone in the team needs to know not just the "what" and the "how" but the "why." This clarity, coupled with a culture where people are held accountable for their results, drives disciplined execution. This is worth repeating (it's that important): *clarity, around the what, how, and why, coupled with accountability, is where disciplined execution lies in a high-performing, scaling company.*

Clarity comes from consistently communicating expectations and the shared understanding of goals. Accountability is then enforced through regular check-ins and the transparent, *consistent* tracking of progress against strategic goals and the business's KPIs. It's really not more complicated than this. We find most companies overcomplicate this, or worse, don't really do it at all. Together, these elements ensure that the organization's path toward scaling goals is both disciplined and dynamically responsive to challenges, which is essential for effective execution.

We covered an entire chapter on processes and systems, so we want to avoid sounding redundant. However, processes as they pertain to managing operations are the backbone of disciplined execution. They provide a clear roadmap, outlining who does what, when, and how. This is not an area to delegate to a project manager, nor is it about copying a template from another company. Rather, it's about creating, documenting, and adhering to an operating management system that works for your specific context and business setting.

A Mini-Case in Operational Excellence Through MOS

Our experience suggests that a company's management operating system (MOS) serves as the backbone of this approach, ensuring a two-way vertical flow of information. Using a recent client, a vibrant consumer goods company, where the issue wasn't that chaos ran supreme, but the entropy caused by the business's built-up complexities was preventing it from getting important projects done. After carefully evaluating the existing framework, we were able to recommend and implement a simple but effective management operating system.

This system primarily revolved around a series of structured key communication practices: it began with an annual offsite strategic planning meeting, which established the direction for the upcoming year. That was followed by quarterly strategic updates to review progress and adjust the approach. Then, weekly leadership updates ensured all executives were on the same page. One-on-one sync-ups, every other week, also encouraged individual accountability and open communication. Finally, weekly and daily team planning meetings, which were transcribed and managed through Asana (a technology software), drove the necessary day-to-day actions to achieve these goals.

The system wasn't overly complex (and shouldn't need to be), yet it had an immediate impact. It took the team about 90 days to fully adapt. Fortunately, after spending so much time feeling the pain of inefficiency, the team knew a structured approach like this was long overdue. Thus, adoption was well received. Keep in mind, though, this is not always the case. Some companies, or people rather, might be less receptive to implementing an MOS or transitioning from their existing systems. In such scenarios, it's crucial to align the team, gain full buy-in, and highlight the value and improved quality of work life of an MOS.

Sometimes, it requires a significant effort—with an extra push from the top—to get it implemented. Once in motion, however, maintaining the regular cadence of the MOS is where most leaders tend to struggle, leading to a loss in execution momentum. It is challenging initially, akin to getting a giant flywheel to begin to turn, and it requires a tremendous amount of effort to overcome the initial inertia. But once the flywheel of disciplined execution starts to spin, it continues to turn faster and easier over time.

The discipline and rigor of your operating system are critical not just for maintaining routine but for embedding the execution into the fabric of the organization. These regular interactions are not merely procedural check-ins but are crucial for building team trust and peer-to-peer accountability while serving as platforms for over-communicating the why behind actions, which is essential for meaningful engagement and coherence across the company.

Moreover, these structured meetings and updates enable team members to develop the emotional fortitude necessary for collaborative problem-solving to move without haste. They encourage individuals to take initiative and proactively work on solutions—*acting with intention*—ingraining these behaviors as values and cultural norms rather than obligations imposed from above. The key, once again, is the discipline to uphold the meetings while holding people accountable.

Leadership: Maintaining Discipline During Rapid Growth

As your business scales, maintaining discipline can, and will, be the most challenging part. New people, processes, and priorities emerge, often creating a complex web leading to organizational friction, called entropy, that can dilute the original discipline that sets you on the path of growth.

At the heart of disciplined execution will be *your* own leadership methodology. Leaders who embody and re-enforce discipline inspire their teams to adhere to established processes within the management operating system, as they strive for excellence.

This type of leadership involves leading by example—demonstrating commitment to the organization's values through daily actions, not just verbal queues. It also consists of communicating the importance of discipline in meetings, processes, and performance management, making it clear that these are not bureaucratic necessities but vital elements of the company's path to scaling success.

In our experience, disciplined leadership is not about being authoritarian. Rather, it's about fostering an environment where discipline is valued and rewarded. Leaders who balance empathy with expectations tend to cultivate the most disciplined teams. They understand that discipline is not just about following processes. It's about commitment to a shared vision and mutual respect for each team member's role in achieving it.

By consistently modeling and upholding these standards, you cultivate an environment where excellence is achieved through standardized processes coupled with continuous improvement.

Creating a culture that celebrates and practices discipline ensures that the organization can grow without diluting its purpose or performance standards. As you scale, this culture becomes your company's internal driving force, supporting every step of growth and ensuring your scaling efforts are as effective as they are ambitious.

Areas Where Discipline Usually Falters

There are plenty of ways discipline can slip. The most common, in our experience, are:

- the discipline to hold managers and leaders accountable;
- the discipline to ensure every meeting happens, and ends, on time;
- the discipline to follow processes, even when you've done the task a thousand times before;
- the discipline to rigorously measure, report, and hold your people accountable to KPIs;
- the discipline to practice delayed gratification in spending, especially when hiring expensive talent;
- the discipline to listen to customer feedback, and act on it;
- the discipline to vigorously defend your culture.

Having the courage and leadership fortitude to instill a culture of discipline while being the type of leader who leads by example is key to continuous scaling without falling apart. Here's a deeper look into each of the facets of discipline that are critical for effective execution:

Managerial Accountability

This involves creating a culture where accountability is valued and enforced. It means setting clear expectations for managers and leaders and then regularly reviewing their performance against these benchmarks. It's not just about tracking outcomes but also about providing the guidance and support needed to achieve the desired impact. Feedback should be welcomed by all, from all peers, and received with an assumption of positive intent as an opportunity to find room for improvement.

Timeliness in Meetings

Discipline often shows in the small details. Meetings that start and end on time are a sign of respect for everyone's time and a marker of operational efficiency. This practice helps instill a broader culture of punctuality and respect for schedules throughout the organization.

Process Adherence

As operations become routine, there's a temptation to cut corners. Maintaining discipline in following established processes ensures that quality and standards do not degrade as the company grows. This consistency is key to scaling because it stabilizes your business's outputs and reliability.

KPI Enforcement

Key performance indicators (KPIs) are essential tools for measuring progress and efficiency. Assuming the right ones have been chosen, rigorous measurement, reporting, and enforcement of KPIs ensure that everyone in the organization understands their goals and the metrics by which they are evaluated. This clarity helps align efforts and prioritize actions that drive continuity and business growth.

Spending Discipline

Financial prudence, especially in scaling phases, is crucial. Discipline in spending means making strategic choices about where to allocate resources, particularly in hiring and investments. Practicing delayed gratification, or pursuing only high return on investment projects, by prioritizing essential expenditures can safeguard financial health and support sustainable growth.

Customer Feedback

As rudimentary as it sounds, this involves not only gathering customer feedback but also integrating it meaningfully into business operations and product development. By actively responding to customer insights, a company demonstrates its commitment to continual product improvement and customer satisfaction, which are important for long-term success and scalability.

Defending Culture

This discipline entails quite possibly the most challenging of all: up-holding the core values and behaviors that define your company, even in the face of rapid growth or external pressures. By defending its culture, a leader that ensures its foundational principles remain intact, fostering a consistent, unified, and productive work environment lends itself to a more sustainable, and personally fulfilling, scaling journey.

The Discipline Audit

To ensure these disciplines remain intact and to find ways to improve them, a tactic I've long employed, and we recommend to our clients, is the "Discipline Audit." Start by assigning each of these disciplines to individual leaders. Then, at least once per month, within their leadership one-on-one meetings, we focus our conversation around those areas within our processes, communication channels, and decision-making structures where discipline might be slipping. So, we can discuss immediate ways to take corrective action. These regular check-ins and resulting continuous improvements help keep the organization aligned and disciplined, even amidst rapid growth.

Here's a short story that illustrates the power of disciplined execu-tion, regardless of the size of your organization or how busy you might be...

Mini-Case in Operational Excellence: A Daily Commitment to Discipline

At QuickBox, our third-party logistics (3PL) company, we faced the monumental task of processing over 30,000 orders daily. This involved pulling hundreds of thousands of pieces each day to assemble into orders, all on behalf of our clients. These orders had to be processed by the local cut-off time, seven days a week, 365 days a year. We accomplished this by operating with over 500 employees across nearly 60 separate business units spread over three warehouse locations.

Given the scale of our operations, it would be easy to assume that we didn't have the time for meetings, let alone daily ones. However, we strongly believed that regular communication was essential for maintaining efficiency, velocity, and excellence. That's why we implemented "daily huddle planning meetings" by business units, every single morning, without fail.

Each business unit had a team leader responsible for sharing critical information, presenting the day's plan, and setting daily goals. They also addressed any obstacles, such as limited staff, the need for flexible staffing, or inventory shortages. This routine gave our team the flexibility to adjust their plans as needed, ensuring we could meet our daily targets despite any challenges.

These daily planning meetings were non-negotiable. Even if only two people were present, the meeting took place. Our commitment to this practice, along with other regular team weekly meetings, including our owners' Wednesday sessions, formed the backbone of our operations. In fact, we never missed an owners' meeting for almost five years until we sold the company.

The consistency and transparency fostered by these meetings ensured that everyone was on the same page, problems were swiftly addressed, and the team remained motivated and aligned with our goals. The *rigor* and *discipline* to uphold these daily meetings were critical. They allowed us to maintain operational excellence and ultimately outpace our competitors.

Our experience at QuickBox taught us that no matter how "large" or "busy" your organization is, prioritizing the discipline to regular communication is key to scaling successfully. We found it fostered a culture of accountability, transparency, and continuous improvement, which were all vital for sustaining our hyper-growth pace and staying ahead in a highly competitive market. This disciplined approach not only helped us manage the complexities of our operations but also played, I strongly believe, a significant role in our success and scalable growth.

~

In summary, discipline in scaling is about more than just rules and regulations. It's about creating a culture that values clarity, accountability, and consistency. It's about empowering rather than inhibiting. And, most importantly, it's about leadership that inspires and upholds discipline, not as a means of control but as a pathway to freedom—freedom to improve, grow, scale, and succeed while staying true to the values of your business. Make no mistake, upholding discipline is what separates companies that scale successfully from those that stumble.

We'll leave this chapter with a last bit of advice: that is, whenever you find yourself in a whirlwind of rapid growth and things feel stuck, or your team is working harder, yet you're not seeing the results materialize, ask yourself: *Is our discipline keeping pace?* Because without discipline, as you scale, so does the chaos. It feels exciting but is ultimately unsustainable.

Let's now turn our attention to the words found in the subtitle of our book and focus on how to preserve your soul while you scale...

Chapter 12

Preserving Your Soul While Scaling Your Business

The foundation of every scaling company is its soul. The essence of why it was created in the first place. It's the moral fibers, ethical compass, purpose, and values that bind together to form the company's indelible soul.

In the heady rush to scale a business, it's all too easy to lose sight of the very reasons that sparked your company's journey. This chapter explores the vital practice of preserving your soul—corporately and personally— amidst the whirlwind of rapid growth, ensuring your business scales not just in size but in character and depth, *and* equally important, that you keep your sanity.

Holding Onto Your "Why"

When you first decided to launch your venture, there was undoubt-edly a powerful reason—a vision or a mission that pulled you for-ward. It might have been a desire to change the industry, revolution-ize a product, or simply do something that matters deeply to you. As your business grows, the challenge isn't just to increase numbers—it's to amplify impact without diluting the essence of your original vision.

The "why" of your business is a large part of its soul. As you scale, every decision, pivot, or tactical move should be measured against this why. It's easy to get sidetracked by the day-to-day demands or the shiny new opportunities that promise faster growth. As Mark Cuban so profoundly says, "It's easy to drown in opportunities."

However, real success lies in alignment with your foundational mis-sion. That's because, at its core, scaling is not just about hitting fi-nancial targets or key numerical metrics. Rather, it's about expand-ing the reach and impact of your core mission without losing sight of what made you start in the first place.

Sustaining Core Values in Times of Change

If your business's why is its soul, then your values are its feet. I realize this sounds a bit corny, but consider for a moment how feet need to stay grounded. The values are the principles that guide how you operate, make decisions, and interact with customers and team members. Your values are the constants that usually *don't* change, despite an ever-changing world and sometimes tumultuous landscape.

Even as strategies shift, goals change, and business models pivot, your values should remain untouched by the whims of market trends or the allure of short-sighted gains. Unless, of course, the value was originally developed merely to espouse, but the company finds that it doesn't reinforce it or actually live it out in their day-to-day interactions. In that case, it may need to change in favor of something the company is more aligned with or even remove it altogether.

As you bring new people into your organization, it's super important to integrate individuals who resonate and align with these core values. The right team members can be your greatest asset, not just for their skills but also for their alignment with your vision, values, and ethos. A team that shares a common set of values is more cohesive, resilient, and according to research, twice as motivated to contribute to a shared goal.

Knowing When to Walk Away: A Mini-Case in Preserving Your Soul When a Business Is at Stake

When co-founding Parka Products, our mission was clear: to solve battery performance degradation in freezing temperatures by creating specialized heated cases for electronic devices. We aimed to make it easier to stay connected outdoors and address safety issues. During the startup phase, we developed the product and navigated the intellectual property process. Our phone case was nearly ready for manufacturing, and we had plans to launch it the following winter.

However, our progress hit a significant roadblock when the patent office notified us that another patent—identical to ours—had already been approved (called prior art). Realizing the gravity of the situation, I reached out to the patent holder, Mr. Clark of Arctic Electronics (a fictitious company name for confidentiality purposes), to explore collaboration. We negotiated an agreement to work together, with us handling direct-to-consumer sales and government contracts while he focused on B2B opportunities.

Feeling optimistic, I introduced our project to a venture capitalist. However, after two weeks of silence, I received an alarming email from Mr. Clark. His disrespectful demeanor made me immediately pause and question the values and professionalism of the people we were potentially going to work with.

The following day, I called Mr. Clark to discuss the email and our next steps. Unfortunately, the conversation became heated. Mr. Clark accused us of excluding him from important discussions and even called us "government spies" trying to steal his patent. This conversation, followed by other similar interactions, led me to believe his aggressive and erratic behavior was a clear signal of how he might treat others in the future.

It became evident that continuing the partnership would be untenable. Despite the potential financial benefits, I realized that aligning with individuals who did not share my values and professional standards was a path I would not venture. Walking away from Parka Products felt like abandoning a part of myself, but deep down, I knew it was the *right* decision.

This experience taught me the invaluable lesson that maintaining your soul and authenticity is vital, even in the face of promising business opportunities. Success should never come at the cost of compromising one's values. There will always be other opportunities, but being mindful of those you associate with, protecting your soul, and living in a sustainable manner is paramount.

The Most Important Question of Them All: Raison d'être

During every journey we've encountered in scaling a business, I can assure you there will come a pivotal moment—a silent interlude amidst the organizational chaos—when revisiting the very essence of your existence as a company becomes not just beneficial but critically essential.

As a business owner, this introspection involves delving deep into the core question:

"Why does my business exist?"

The answer lies far beyond the surface-level metrics of revenue and profit. It probes into the problem you initially set out to solve and how this mission intertwines with your deepest values and reason for existing.

When pondering this question, consider the inception of your idea. It likely started with a spark—an observation of a gap or a need that was unmet by the current market. This gap, your niche, is where your business's soul begins to take shape. It's not merely about what your product or service does, it's also about the satisfaction it brings to your customers, the ease in which it intertwines into their lives, and the incredible joy it might provide its users.

Your business's raison d'être (a French term meaning the most important reason or purpose for someone or something's existence) should resonate with a mission that goes beyond transactions. It should reflect a purpose that impacts your customer community, the industry at large, or a cause you feel strongly about supporting.

This foundational mission serves as your guiding star on the tumultuous sea of business scaling. It helps you navigate through decisions that, if made with the improper drivers, could potentially dilute your brand's essence or lead you astray from your original path. Every strategic move, every innovation, every new employee you add to your team, and every market expansion initiative should be in alignment with and a reflection of this mission, ensuring that growth never comes at the expense of your core reason for being.

By anchoring your scaling efforts in the deep-seated reasons for your business's existence, you are safeguarding the integrity of your company's soul. This not only resonates with your employees, giving them a greater sense of purpose in their work, but it also builds deeper trust with your customers. They aren't just investing in a product or service; they're endorsing a mission. They're supporting a vision of the world that aligns with their values. Remember, people might forget what you said, but they will never forget how you made them feel—this is the essence of a business soul that thrives through the stages of growth.

Finding Purpose

It's important to note, however, that discovering your mission might not be a foundational moment but rather an organic evolution like we experienced at QuickBox. (Recall back to the chapter on People and our "second-chance" revolution that spawned our mission.) Initially, we were driven by operational goals and bottom-line results, and suddenly, our true purpose emerged unexpectedly from the personal stories and lives of our team members. This pivotal shift occurred when we started offering employment opportunities to those who were often overlooked—those who had faced significant life challenges and were struggling to find a second chance.

The profound impact of this movement transformed QuickBox into a mission-driven company—for our employees and our clients—underscored by the heartfelt stories of employees who had once been without hope and were now thriving. Their gratitude and personal stories not only reshaped our business model but also deeply enriched my life and the corporate culture. This experience illustrates that sometimes, the most impactful mission-driven business transformations arise not from strategic plans but from genuine human connections and the powerful ripple effects they create within and beyond the walls of a company.

Balancing Sanity and Success

Scaling a business is exhilarating, but it's also an emotional and mental rollercoaster. The highs are dizzying, but the lows can be daunting. As the leader in a scaling business, you're likely going to feel the weight of the world on your shoulders. I've been there—watching helplessly as my business partner, overwhelmed by stress, faced a severe mental health crisis. It was a wake-up call for all of us. Thankfully, we had three other co-founders who were talented and compassionate enough to support him through it.

Taking care of your mental and emotional health throughout this journey is as important as any business strategy. If you're not functioning at your best, neither will your business. This means setting boundaries for work and ensuring you have time to unwind and reconnect in your personal life.

For me, this lesson was learned the hard way. In my earlier years, I was so consumed with "building a business" that I neglected my family, leading to the painful end of my first marriage. Since then, I learned how to prioritize time with my loved ones—*it's non-negotiable*—and I'm happily remarried to a spouse who values my work, but we both recognize our time together is more precious.

Just like you schedule meetings and deadlines, schedule time for yourself and your family. It's not just a break; it's an investment in your capacity to lead and grow your business sustainably.

A Story in Soul-Searching

After being involved in, consulting for, and hanging around a vast number of business founders, there are not many we've witnessed who have preserved their souls better than the founders of a company called Mid-Day Squares.

Siblings Jake and Lezlie Karls and Lezlie's husband Nick Saltzman founded Mid-Day Squares in Montreal, Canada. Their company specializes in producing organic, plant-based chocolate snack bars that are as functional and nutritious as they are sweet and delicious.

They've skirted the brink of failure several times and have since scaled into North America's finest retailers like Target, Costco, and Erewhon. What sets Mid-Day Squares apart is not just their tasty, better-for-you chocolate products but their transparent and innovative approach to business. (I'm going to warn you, the cookie dough flavor will addict your taste buds, like it did mine.)

They are known for their candid public sharing on social media of the ups and downs of their entrepreneurial journey.

I met with Jake Karls to talk about how they've successfully navigated nurturing their souls through the course of scaling their better-for-you chocolate company. Aside from being an optimist at heart (much like myself), Jake is wiser in business acumen than his aged years and an absolute pleasure to talk with. Here is their story...

A Mini-Case in Protecting Your Soul While Scaling a Business: The Mid-Day Squares Journey

When Jake Karls co-founded Mid-Day Squares, he and his partners established a set of core values that would serve as the foundation for their business. These values were more than just words on a wall. They were principles that guided every decision and action. One key value was to "be right more than you are wrong," encouraging the team to take risks and learn from their mistakes.

Initially, they also embraced "always good vibes" but realized it created undue pressure, so they evolved it to encourage authentic positivity. These core values were integral during the startup and growth phases, guiding hiring processes and ensuring team alignment as they expanded.

Mid-Day Squares faced multiple near-failure moments, including the brink of bankruptcy. During these times, Jake and his team learned the importance of resilience, courage, and the ability to withstand immense pressure.

Instead of playing defense, they shifted to an offensive mindset, making bold decisions and embracing the possibility of failure. This approach allowed them to navigate legal battles, financial challenges, and operational hurdles, ultimately turning potential failures into opportunities for growth.

To handle the pressures of not failing, especially in the early stages, Jake and his partners committed to weekly therapy sessions. These sessions, regardless of whether times were good or bad, helped them become better leaders, business partners, and maintain their mental health. Building a strong team was also crucial: they hired talented individuals, delegated responsibilities, and stayed focused on their strengths. Therapy taught them to have difficult conversations and listen actively, improving decision-making and team dynamics.

As Mid-Day Squares grew, ensuring every decision aligned with their core values became even more critical. Acting quickly and decisively, especially regarding team dynamics, was essential. If a team member no longer aligned with their values, they addressed it promptly. In the past, they had held onto misaligned team members out of fear, causing long-term issues. Now, they prioritize what's best for the organization, maintaining harmony and effectiveness.

Therapy has been a cornerstone of Mid-Day Squares' success. It taught the team to be vulnerable and transparent, fostering open communication and resolving conflicts more effectively. Through therapy, they learned to have tough conversations, actively listen, and understand each other better. This practice has strengthened their partnership and leadership, allowing them to navigate the challenges of scaling a business together. It's a lifelong commitment they believe is essential for maintaining mental health and team cohesion.

Despite the inevitable shifts and changes that come with business growth, Mid-Day Squares has remained true to its initial vision. This means continuously revisiting their core values and ensuring they guide every decision. By focusing on their mission and the unique value they bring to customers, they navigate changes and stay aligned with their original goals.

For Jake, a company's soul is defined by its humanization—the way it connects with people on a personal level. (For the record, this is probably the simplest and most profound definition of a company's soul, and I told Jake I was going to borrow this phrase.) At Mid-Day Squares, this means being authentic and transparent and maintaining their core values in every aspect of the business. By staying true to who they are and focusing on their mission, they've preserved their soul through all the ups and downs.

Jake emphasizes that the journey of entrepreneurship, while rewarding, is filled with challenges and is far from glamorous. It's essential
to focus on your vision and values rather than getting caught up in
external noise. Success requires resilience, courage, and the ability to
withstand pressure. Instead of chasing superficial success, Jake ad-
vises entrepreneurs to build meaningful and sustainable businesses.

Jake's advice to other entrepreneurs is to stay true to their core values, build a strong team, and prioritize mental health. Tools like
therapy can help navigate the emotional and psychological challenges of entrepreneurship. Staying focused on the vision, obsessing
over the customer experience, and not getting distracted by external
noise are crucial. Building a successful business is a long-term journey, and maintaining your soul is key to enduring the challenges
along the way.

Mid-Day Squares exemplifies how maintaining core values, fostering open communication, and integrating therapy can preserve a
company's soul while scaling, offering a powerful lesson on sustain-
ing authenticity and resilience amidst rapid growth.

Nurturing Your Soul *and* Your Business

As your business scales, the landscape around you will undeniably
change, yet the core of what makes your company uniquely yours
should stand immutable amidst this evolution. It's for this reason it
is vital to erect and maintain firm boundaries around the elements

most integral to your identity—your values, your time, and your personal well-being.

These boundaries aren't merely defensive walls. Rather, they serve as a shield to the foundational stones of your venture that will not only climb the peaks of market success but also remain authentic and resonant with your original vision.

Consider your personal values as the compass that guides your business decisions through the stormy seas of growth. These values have likely always been clear to you. However, as success grows and pressures mount, there's a temptation to bend these principles for expedient gains. *Resist this temptation at all costs.* Maintaining your integrity with personal values isn't just about ethics. It's about creating a personal brand that stands for something—with a leader people can trust and feel connected to.

When I was the CEO of a public company, there was a pervasive saying on Wall Street: "You're only as good as your last quarter." This adage underscored a harsh reality—leadership and company performance were judged solely on one criterion: quarterly earnings. The expectation was unyielding—each quarter's results had to surpass the last.

While a company should certainly yield value to its stakeholders, I detested the relentless pressure from shareholders and Wall Street, which made it painfully clear that producing earnings at all costs was the only priority. This constant demand forced us into making short-term decisions focused solely on generating immediate profits, often at the expense of long-term gains. Each quarter felt like a stripping away of our company's cultural values, and it took a toll on my soul. The experience taught me a great deal about running a public company, but I found no joy in this relentless cycle. The erosion of my values in the face of such pressure was disheartening. Over time, it became painfully clear: protecting your values is essential to preserving the soul.

Similarly, guarding your time becomes increasingly crucial as demands on it vastly expand. Time management should not solely focus on productivity but also on preserving moments for reflection, creativity, and recovery. This harmony is not just beneficial; it's essential. It prevents burnout, fosters sustained innovation, and keeps you deeply connected to your entrepreneurial spirit.

Lastly, your personal well-being is the wellspring from which your entrepreneurial energy flows. Neglecting it in the race for business growth is akin to draining your venture's most crucial resource. Cultivate it with the same dedication you cultivate your business with. Engage in practices that sustain your mental and physical health, ensuring that as your business grows, you are not diminishing.

By staunchly protecting these aspects of your entrepreneurial journey, you stand at the helm of a thriving business that doesn't just grow in scale but grows in depth and resilience. Remember, a company that reflects the best of its founders' intentions and values is an inspiration in its market—one that attracts loyal customers and dedicated employees alike.

The Amazing Scaling Race

Scaling a business is more like the television show *The Amazing Race* than it is a sprint or a marathon. Crossing the finish line in our amazing race to scale your business will be a moment of triumph that transcends the mere metrics of your success. It will become a profound testament to your journey—not just to what you've built but to who you've evolved into along the way.

We'll avoid measuring your success by what you see on social media or read online when a tech unicorn hits a billion-dollar valuation. Because each person and every company has their own unique journey, their own timeline, and their own metrics of success. We'll focus on *your* path and define success on your *own* terms.

Trust me when I say that this achievement is as much about your personal growth as it is about the growth of your company. When you are able to navigate this challenging landscape without compromising the values that define you, the victory is particularly sweet. It's a confirmation that success doesn't require a sacrifice of identity, or your soul, but can actually emerge from its emphatic expression.

This ultimate achievement will speak volumes. It will tell the story of a leader who didn't just chase after profits but sought to enrich lives and make a genuine difference in the world. It will reflect a business that has grown not only in size but in purpose and impact. As you stand at this precipice, what you will have managed to preserve and enhance within your core identity will be as commendable as the business empire you'll have built.

When looking back, let this milestone be a mirror, reflecting you, as a leader, who has thrived through challenges without diluting their soul. Remember, the most inspiring tales of success are those where leaders not only reach their targets but also uplift their teams, delight their customers, and positively impact their communities—all while staying true to themselves.

Make no mistake, this is *your* legacy—a booming business that carries a piece of your soul in its blueprint and a personal transformation that speaks to the power of leading with authenticity and purpose. We will celebrate not only the empire you've built but also the person you've become throughout this formidable journey.

As we begin to wrap up our time together...

Let us remember that scaling your business while preserving your soul isn't just a lofty goal or a slogan on the front cover of a book—it's the most authentic path to success. Staying true to your "why," steadfast in your values, and mindful of your well-being is the ultimate test of every entrepreneur's scaling journey. And while you might not travel through it unscathed, by protecting these aspects of yourself and your business, you will make it through with your soul intact. Before we move on to pulling everything together and putting our scaling principles into action, we'd like to first dispel the most common myths surrounding scaling...

Chapter 13

Scaling Myths Debunked: Separating Fact from Fiction

Within the entrepreneurship ecosystem, myths about scaling a business are as abundant and embellished as any piece of classic folklore. Adding to the challenge, the rise of the "Instagram entrepreneur"—often depicted in glamorous snapshots of hustle and living the good life—has distorted these myths even further. Many of these social media moguls showcase a lifestyle of achievement without substantiating their claims with real business success, particularly the kind that involves scaling a company to respectable revenues. This phenomenon has not only perpetuated existing myths but has also created new ones, misleading many aspiring entrepreneurs about what it truly takes to scale a business effectively.

While these stories can be entertaining, believing in them without a critical examination poses significant risks. Myths can mislead founders into adopting strategies that are not only ineffective but potentially detrimental, diverting resources from proven paths of success.

In this chapter, we will dissect some of the most commonly perpetuated myths and reveal the practical truths. By thoroughly understanding and debunking these myths, you will be well-prepared to navigate away from common entrepreneurial pitfalls and guide your venture with informed clarity and precision.

Let's dive in and debunk some of these myths with a hard dash of reality…

MYTH ONE: Any Business Can Scale

The belief that "any business can scale" is as popular as it is misleading. Scaling is indeed within reach for many of us. However, it's important to acknowledge that while most business models can endure a rapid expansion, not all founders are cut out to handle the pressures of a rapidly scaling business.

Consider your local barber. The founder might wield his scissors with unmatched skill, giving the best haircuts in town. However, if he attempts to take his barbershop national overnight without adapting his business model for scalability, he's likely to encounter unforeseen barriers that will prevent growth. Yet, this doesn't imply the barbershop business model is inherently unscalable. In fact, it could be quite the opposite.

Suppose the barbershop founder perfects his shop's operations, maximizes profitability, and creates a unique experience that has customers clamoring for entry. He could then consider replicating his successful shop in a nearby town or even another city with similar demographics. Gradually, he might expand regionally, then nationally, and perhaps even internationally. Or, he could consider another scalable approach—franchising. This model has scaled numerous local businesses to widespread success.

A prime example of barbershop scaling success is Floyd's 99 Barbershop. Established in 1999 by the O'Brien brothers—Paul, Rob, and Bill—in Denver, Colorado, Floyd's 99 expanded its unique "rock and roll" themed barbershop concept to 119 locations across 13 states. The key to their success? A well-crafted, scalable business model that tapped into a niche market, combined with a strategic growth plan, and team of founders truly committed to the scaling journey.

TRUTH: Business Scale Differs from Founder Scale

Scalability is possible for nearly every business but not every founder. It requires a well-understood and carefully planned path that is adapted to, or modified from, the business model. That being said, a founder who approaches challenges with humility, an eagerness and curiosity to learn, a healthy balance of risk appetite and avoidance, and an open mind can grow into the type of founder who can scale their business. Just like your business, where you are now doesn't have to be where you end up.

MYTH TWO: Scaling is Fun!

There's undeniable excitement in watching your business grow—seeing numbers climb, markets broaden, and your entrepreneurial profile bloom into that of a recognized thought leader. However, equating scaling only with its highs is like expecting a rollercoaster to be nothing but adrenaline-filled speed, drops, and flips.

The reality is that scaling brings its fair share of challenges, and it's downright hard. Teams may feel overwhelmed, operational mishaps will undoubtedly arise, complex problems will need solving, and market dynamics can throw unexpected punches.

The path to scaling isn't a straight, upward trajectory. It often involves working late nights and weekends and managing stress levels that can sometimes feel overwhelming. But ask any entrepreneur who has successfully scaled their business: *Is it worth it?* The resounding answer is yes.

Leading a growing venture through the ups and downs of scaling is immensely rewarding, offering an incredible sense of accomplishment that few other experiences can match.

TRUTH: Brace Yourself

Prepare for all facets of the scaling journey. It's not just about enjoying the exhilarating climbs and popping champagne during the wins. It's also about navigating the inevitable descents and losses with resilience to persist and determination to learn along the way.

Strap in and be ready for the full experience—it is demanding, but overcoming these challenges is even more rewarding than a straight line to the top. It's in overcoming these difficulties that we learn the most, grow personally and professionally, and prove to ourselves what we are capable of. It's when we realize that with the right people and a well-built and communicated plan, we can be next to unstoppable.

MYTH THREE: Burn Rate Is Directly Proportional to Growth Rate

In the high-octane world of VC-funded startups, there's a commonly perpetrated belief that burning cash at a high rate is synonymous with rapid growth. But using excessive funds without seeing equivalent growth is like burning a puddle of gasoline.

Once the fuel is exhausted, nothing remains to keep the fire burning, and the cold, dark night will soon close in on your party. Indeed, growth consumes capital, often voraciously, but this doesn't justify a cavalier attitude toward financial mismanagement.

A wisely scaling business can often fund much of its growth internally, and when external capital is involved, it should be deployed with strategic precision. True scaling efficiency occurs when revenue growth hits an inflection point and begins increasing at a rate disproportionate to operating expenses. This is the essence of real scaling and should be the aim of every entrepreneur on their scaling journey. Falling into the mindset that a hefty bank balance (courtesy of investors or significant fundraising) necessitates extravagant spending is a trap.

TRUTH: Value Efficiency Over Expenditure

Make sure every dollar you spend works as hard as you do. Efficient use of capital resources often outweighs the benefits of simply increasing expenditures. The key is not to spend more but to spend intelligently with the same return on that capital that any investor would want to see. Remember, fundraising often becomes a full-time job on its own. The less time you can spend chasing money, the more time you can focus on improving your business and building enterprise value.

MYTH FOUR: Scaling Is Synonymous with Profit

The notion that scaling automatically equates to immediate profitability is a tempting but only partial truth.

Consider the journey of Amazon, which, despite its current behemoth status, did not see a profit until *nine years after its inception*. Scaling involves significant investment, and the financial returns might not materialize swiftly. That said, not every business could withstand being unprofitable for that duration. What's critical to remember is that profit does not always translate directly into cash. In the scaling phase, as we discussed earlier, the focus should predominantly be on managing cash flow effectively to support ongoing growth.

However, it is also true that scaling within a high-margin framework can lead to considerable profits. The ability to scale should, in theory, amplify profitability. As my first CFO, Bruce, often reminded me, "Remember, you don't take percentages to the bank; you deposit dollars." He emphasized that a diligent focus on actual profit dollars, rather than mere profit percentages, is an imperative distinction for substantial and healthy growth—and it certainly helps you sleep better at night.

TRUTH: Cultivate Patience; Reap Rewards

Embrace patience and focus on short-term decisions that affect the *cash flow* in the business, which are more likely to yield long-term returns, rather than chasing immediate gains that may present a higher risk to the company. This approach not only ensures steady growth but also fortifies the financial health of your business over time.

MYTH FIVE: Scaling Happens by Luck

The idea that scaling a business is a product of sheer luck might make for an enchanting Cinderella story, but in reality, successful scaling is far from a fairy tale. It doesn't hinge on happenstance or piecing together the latest growth hacks, but rather on a disciplined, principles-centered approach that demands an in-depth understanding of your business, the market, and product or service with a clear competitive advantage. True scaling involves navigating through complex challenges and requires an enduring commitment to your vision, values, and goals.

The adage that "luck is what happens when preparation meets opportunity" is particularly apt in the context of business scaling. If we accept this definition, then scaling is not a product of luck but the result of meticulous preparation and the ability to seize the right opportunities at the right time. Any other notion of luck has little to no role in the deliberate and strategic process of scaling a business. Unless, of course, your product gets surprisingly highlighted by a massive celebrity. But even then, this momentum is usually impossible to sustain.

TRUTH: You Forge Your Own Path to Success

Don't sit back and wait for hope, prayer, or luck to transform your business overnight. Lace up your boots, arm yourself with a solid plan, and carve out your own success story. Scaling is about more than just understanding your business and the market; it's about wholeheartedly believing in your vision and relentlessly pursuing it. It's the courage to face complex challenges that come with scaling, along with the determination to stay true to your values.

True success comes not from being "lucky" but from meticulous preparation and seizing the right opportunities at the right time. Remember, every step you take during this journey brings you closer to your goal. Embrace the journey, stay committed, and let your passion drive you. By embracing our scaling principles and putting in the hard work, you can (and will!) forge your own path to extraordinary success.

In conclusion, while myths can be entertaining, they shouldn't be the guiding force behind your scaling ambition, nor should their half-baked truths hold you back. It's time to create a scaling story that other entrepreneurs will look up to—minus the myths. Together, we will embark on this journey toward genuinely meaningful and substantial scaling, firmly rooted in the realities of our proven framework.

Now it's time to turn our attention to the final chapter, where we're going to put together everything we've learned so far and lay out the first five steps you can take to start *your* scaling journey…

Chapter 14

Putting It All Together—Readiness to Scale

We've arrived at that point in our journey where it's time for you to ask: *"What's next?"*

Because scaling isn't just about expanding your business—it's about doing so intentionally, efficiently, and, yes, rapidly. And so, without hesitation, it's time for us to take what you've learned within *Ready, Set, SCALE*, and put it into action. It's time to prepare your business for the adventure of scaling.

Let's start by focusing on the next five steps you can take after studying (and, with some hard work, mastering) our principles so you can achieve significant strides toward scaling *your* business.

STEP 1. Understand Your "Why"

Before diving headfirst into our scaling journey, we encourage you to take a moment to step back and ask the fundamental question: *"Why do I want to scale?"*

This introspective inquiry is critical as it grounds your scaling journey in purpose and clarity. Are you aiming to generate ongoing profits, expand market reach and impact, secure a legacy, build a business to pass along to your children, bring fame to yourself, or build enterprise value so you can eventually sell your company? There are no wrong answers. It's your answer; it's personal. Understanding your underlying motivations will guide your strategic decisions, making them more focused and an effective driving force as you lead this charge.

Begin this exploration by documenting your longer-term personal and business goals, both intrinsic and extrinsic. Reflect on what you hope to achieve through scaling—be it financial security, innovation, influence, fame, or a combination of these. This clarity will not only fuel your ambition but also serve as a compass when faced with tough choices.

Remember, scaling is not just a business decision; it's a mindful commitment to carrying forward a vision that aligns with your deepest aspirations. By anchoring your scaling efforts in a well-defined "why," you'll ensure your business growth is meaningful and aligned with your values and goals. This foundation will not only motivate you but will also resonate with your team, investors, and customers, creating a shared sense of purpose and direction.

STEP 2. Identify Your Business Lifecycle Stage

Our next step is to focus on identifying where your business currently stands in its lifecycle. This is not a typical business lifecycle bell curve you would find in a textbook. Rather, it's about understanding where your business lies within the context of reaching the "Level Four" stage of your growth journey, where you're *ready* for scaling. This should ultimately guide where your actions are focused as you get ready to scale.

Level 1 – Start-Up Stage

This initial phase is all about setting up the basics—registering with the state, securing your domain, drafting an operating agreement, and perhaps developing a prototype. At this stage, most businesses are pre-revenue, focused on laying down the structural groundwork to support future activities. This is normally a time of exciting beginnings and setting the stage for what's to come.

Level 2 – Get-Up Stage

Here's where things start to get real. You're moving past the preliminary setup and taking your business live. Whether opening a physical store, gaining an initial purchase order, launching a website, or contracting your first client, this stage is characterized by the first actual sales and extends up until you reach around $1 million in annual trailing revenue. It's about achieving lift-off, setting the foundation with the principles we've covered, and seeing the first signs of market traction by finding product-market fit.

Level 3 – Grow-Up Stage

Often the most challenging phase, this is where businesses strive to cross the significant threshold of $10 million in trailing revenues—or where they find themselves butting up against a revenue ceiling somewhere in between. Many companies falter here, thrown off course or getting stuck while struggling to endure the "growing pains" associated with this stage.

It's a critical time for refining your customer acquisition tactics and ensuring they are sustainable. This stage is about maturing and solidifying your business operations, surrounding the principles we've covered so far, as you prepare for the leap to the next stage. It's about preparing the company's scale readiness for the fourth level of scaling.

Level 4 – Scale-Up Stage

Entering this stage means your business is generating some-where greater than $10 million in trailing revenue and is poised for substantial growth. Preparation in earlier stages comes to fruition here as you fully apply the principles dis-cussed in this book to navigate this expansion successfully.

This is the phase that tests your business's scale readiness and puts everything you've engineered into practice. It's where you put your foot on the pedal and align your team and resources around growth—*hyper-growth*. Scaling up to, and potentially beyond, $100 million in revenues be-comes a tangible goal.

Level 5 – Level-Up Stage (Time to "Double Down")

You've made it! You've reached scaling nirvana. Whether your business surpasses $100 million in trailing revenue or you've reached your scaling financial goal, it enters the "Level Up" stage—ready to "double down" on your scaling principles.

In this phase, it's time to protect your moats and leverage your competitive advantage. This stage focuses on sustain-ing success through continuous innovation and operational refinement to stay ahead of the curve and any competitors.

It's a time to celebrate achievements while strategically exploring new growth avenues—whether that's entering new markets, diversifying product lines, making strategic acquisitions, or contemplating selling your company.

The challenge lies in maintaining your market dominance while planning for future expansions, ensuring the long-term sustainability and the legacy of your business.

STEP 3. Take *The Scale Ready* Self-Assessment

Understanding how the core principles of scaling interlock and support one another is vitally important for building a resilient, scalable business. When you think of scaling, imagine constructing a skyscraper with foundations grounded in bedrock, not a precarious Jenga tower built on a sandbox.

Relying solely on a hodgepodge of growth hacks, social media tips, or the latest tricks and quick fixes will almost always create a shaky foundation that collapses under the slightest bit of pressure from scaling. However, each principle in our framework, whether it's strategy, structure, people, process, or cash, is designed to reinforce your business's scale-readiness architecture.

Skipping steps or ignoring elements can lead to significant constraints that not only stunt growth but could potentially lead to the internal collapse of your company. For example, a robust strategy without the right people to execute it is like having a blueprint without builders. Or, a financial influx without streamlined processes could lead to chaos and wasting money rather than growth. That's why sequence matters—each principle prepares the path for the next, ensuring that the scaling journey is smooth, sustainable, and attainable.

To effectively gauge your readiness for scaling, if you haven't already, consider using our Scale Ready Self-Assessment (refer to Chapter 3 for a more detailed explanation of its value) available at ReadyForScaling.com. Using our proprietary scoring system, this tool is designed to identify any constraints within each of the six areas of the scaling framework that could impede your business's growth potential. It offers detailed insights into the inherent risks of each of the identified constraints and provides guidance on how these issues could be systematically resolved. The Scale Ready Self-Assessment is not just a diagnostic tool. It is a mirror, reflecting the potential scaling bottlenecks in your organization *as it exists today*.

Whether it's a faltered strategy, mismatch in talent or skills, insufficient technology, or capital restrictions, identifying these hurdles is paramount. You'll want to study these findings carefully before prioritizing and taking action on them. By assessing your business's foundation through this lens, you can address and unlock these inhibitors *before* they become critical problems and derail your scaling efforts, setting the stage for robust growth and long-term success with our principles-centered approach.

Access The Scale-Ready Self-Assessment at
ReadyForScaling.com/resources

STEP 4. Share It with Your Team

Effective scaling begins with a unified team. If your scaling journey is a voyage, then your team is your crew. To ensure everyone is on the same page, consider sharing this book with them and, better yet, have them complete the Scale Ready Self-Assessment to see if your team is also aligned in your perspectives.

Whether it's a single partner or a growing staff, providing them with their own copy of *Ready, Set, SCALE* can be instrumental. Encourage them to read and digest the principles laid out within. You could even set up a company "book club" of sorts to digest and discuss each chapter and identify areas to improve as well as successes to celebrate throughout the journey.

This step isn't just about disseminating information—it's about building a common language and understanding, ensuring that every member of your team is equipped and motivated to contribute to a common goal against the backdrop of your intended scaling endeavor. It's about navigating the scaling process together as a unified, purpose-driven team.

Once your team is familiar with the principles of scaling, the next step is to align everyone around the central goals of your expansion. Discuss *why* you want to scale *and* share the insights from your Scale Ready Self-Assessment. This dialogue should cover the specific reasons scaling is critical for your business and the potential benefits and challenges it will bring.

Transparency here is key—ensure *every* team member understands their role and how they will contribute to the journey. This stage is about syncing hearts and minds to a common frequency, turning individual roles into a harmonious team who are committed and ready to rise to the occasion.

STEP 5. Prioritize Actions: Building Your Scale-Ready Action Plan

With your team aligned and informed, it's time to prioritize the actions needed to address any constraints identified in your assessment. In our consulting practice, we rely on a tool we created called The Prioritization Scorecard. This tool provides a framework that distills and simplifies the process of key strategic prioritization.

Access The Prioritization Scorecard at ReadyForScaling.com/resources

The goal of this step is to collaboratively *decide* which barriers to your scaling growth, called constraints, to tackle first based on two criteria: (y) The *level of difficulty* to resolve—formed from its complexity, time to resolve, and allocation of available resources; along with (x) their *level of impact* on the company—based on, once unlocked, its contribution to the financial growth or reduction cost or mitigation of risk, and impact on your business's ability to scale.

This approach not only democratizes the problem-solving process but also leverages diverse perspectives within your team, increasing the likelihood of creative solutions. Trust the process: No matter how wildly complex the problem might appear on the surface, there is a resolution to solve it. Think of it as assembling a puzzle together. Each piece matters, and placing them in the right order accelerates the completion of the picture of your likelihood for success.

Spoiler alert: This won't happen inside an hour-long meeting. It takes careful assessment and mindful collaboration and is often met with spirited debate. It could take a day or two. Nevertheless, this collective prioritization ensures your foundation for scaling is not only rock solid but also supported by *every* team member, making the path to your future growth clear and actionable.

And that's why the final, and most important, part of this step in preparing your team for scaling involves crafting a detailed, actionable plan that outlines each step of the process, complete with timelines, designated responsibilities, and specific actions. This plan serves as your roadmap, detailing who does what and by when, ensuring accountability and clarity across your team.

Start by breaking down the larger goals into manageable tasks and assign each task to a team member best suited for it. Setting clear deadlines and expected outcomes helps keep everyone on track and focused. Make this the first item on the agenda when you meet with your leadership team to discuss each week.

This methodical approach not only streamlines efforts but also empowers your team members by clearly defining their roles in the company's growth trajectory. Like the captain of a ship setting the course, your scale-readiness plan should chart the path from where you are now to where you need to be, turning your scaling ambitions into reality.

Access The Strategic Roadmap to memorialize your action plans at ReadyForScaling.com/resources

Before you dive in, it's worth considering perhaps the most challenging aspect of scaling relative to you and your team. The harsh reality is that you must continue to operate the business *during* your scale-readiness transition.

You don't get the luxury of pausing operations. You must "change the engines while the plane is flying." Said another way, while you're working diligently to unlock the constraints within your business, mastering the principles outlined in our framework, you must simultaneously keep your operations running smoothly and maintain the quality of your product or service. This balancing act requires meticulous planning, unwavering focus, and an adaptable mindset to ensure your business sets itself up for scaling success but doesn't break the company's spirit.

For this reason, we highly encourage you (and your team) to use the tools we laid out within the context of the principles we've shared—they can be found by scanning the code with your smartphone camera or following the URL. We made these tools *free* to those who have a copy of this book in their hands, and we are certain you will find an immense amount of value in leveraging them to help translate the principles into action within each particular area of your business.

Access All of the Tools at ReadyForScaling.com/resources

Sequence Matters

Initiating the scaling process isn't just about pushing the accelerator. It's about understanding the right order of operations—*sequencing*. Sequencing in business scaling is akin to *mise en place,* a common term in cooking, which refers to the practice of preparing and organizing all the ingredients and tools needed for cooking before starting to cook.

The goal is to have everything ready and easily accessible, allowing for a smoother and more efficient cooking process. Similar to an engineer having all their drawings in place and compliant *before* beginning to build a skyscraper, it sets the stage for efficiency and a successful outcome.

That said, we'd be remiss if we failed to highlight the importance of sequencing in our scaling framework—strategy, structure, people, process, and cash. Intensely and diligently focusing on each one—*in that order*—to ensure it's scale-ready. That's because we've found the tendency is to tackle the easiest area of concern, or the one most impeding the business, first. Following our sequence, however, ensures that each element supports the next, creating a cohesive and sustainable scaling journey. This sequence isn't arbitrary. It's a deliberate pathway to ensure each constraint is unlocked and each area of your business is scale-ready before moving to the next. Remember, the strength of your scaling effort lies not just in the individual components but in how well they are integrated and sequenced.

Our Shared Journey of Scaling: This Is Just the Beginning

As we near the conclusion of our journey through the pages of *Ready, Set, SCALE*, it's important to reflect on the principles we've explored together. These lessons, honed and validated through their application in countless businesses, including yours truly, are not mere theories but practical, actionable principles designed to propel your business to new heights. The success stories from clients who've embraced these principles are a testament to their effectiveness—guiding the rewarding path to scaling.

Yet, this book is far from the final chapter in our adventure together. Consider it merely the prelude to an ongoing dialogue among peers driven by a common mission—to scale while retaining our soul.

I invite you to continue this conversation with us. Connect with us on LinkedIn, subscribe to our weekly newsletter at ReadyForScaling.com, and join our community of like-minded entrepreneurs on Slack at #readySetSCALE.

Together, as a collective of forward-thinkers and relentless doers, we can traverse the exciting landscape of scaling. Our journey is continuous and universal, and every step you take enriches this shared path we are treading as we work to build a better world for ourselves and for those who come after us.

Let us leave you with a final story that encapsulates the essence of our scaling philosophy. At my prior company, we embarked on a journey that seemed daunting at first—a quest to scale beyond $100 million in less than five years—with zero industry experience and no outside funding.

By establishing a clear and compelling **strategy**, creating a highly adaptable **structure**, recruiting world-class **people**, implementing robust yet agile **processes and leveraging technology**, and internally **funding** our growth, we turned that ambitious vision into a resounding reality—while revitalizing a local workforce often labeled as "unemployable," producing a newfound mission for our company. This story isn't just about financial metrics or business expansion. It's about the power of disciplined execution and steadfast commitment to a vision.

It's a narrative that illustrates what's possible when you align every aspect of your scale-ready business with its ultimate goals, maintaining a laser focus on not just where you want to go but also on the values that define who you are as an individual and a company.

In your business, as it was in ours, remember: getting strategy, structure, people, process, and cash right isn't just about scaling up, it's about creating something invaluable that is *capable* of scaling. It's about proving that achieving business success and preserving your soul are not just parallel tracks but intertwined paths leading to making an extraordinary impact.

Let our journey, and the many stories of other business owners found throughout the chapters of this book, inspire you, guide you and empower you. If they can do it, so can you.

Here's to getting it right and scaling not just successfully but without losing your soul.

Stephen & Zach

Resources: Unlock Your Scaling Potential

As a token of our gratitude for being a valued reader and scaling community member, we've compiled a repository of the proprietary tools discussed in this book. These tools are our way of helping you effectively implement our scaling framework into your business. Thank you for joining us on this journey. Here are the tools, listed in the order they appear within the chapters:

Take the Scale-Ready Self-Assessment

See if your company's ready to scale; unlock the constraints to your full potential.

→ https://readyforscaling.com/scale-ready-audit

Build Your Strategic Roadmap

Develop your own clear, compelling, and memorable strategy on a single page.

→ readyforscaling.com/resources/strategic-roadmap

Discover The Team Impact Evaluator

Intimately assess, and plot, existing and prospective employees to drive impact, potential, and cultural fit.

→ readyforscaling.com/resources/team-impact-evaluator

Optimize Your Operations with The Ultimate Tech Stack

Massively improve operational velocity by automating key processes with optimal technology software.

→ readyforscaling.com/resources/The-Ultimate-Tech-Stack

Implement the Cash Flow Compass

Forecast your cash to seize opportunities and avoid unexpected surprises.

→ readyforscaling.com/resources/Cash-Flow-Compass

7 Levers Cash Navigator

Take control of the seven levers and optimize your available cash flow to fuel your growth.

→ readyforscaling.com/resources/7-Levers-Cash-Navigator

The Diamond Strategic Positioning Grid

Secure your product's sustainable competitive advantage, now and in the future.

→ readyforscaling.com/resources/Diamond-Strategic-Positioning-Grid

Maximize Impact with the Prioritization Scorecard

Reduce conflict and more easily prioritize key projects based on impact and difficulty.

→ readyforscaling.com/resources/Prioritization-Scorecard

Get In Touch with Us

$\rightarrow$ Reach out to us on LinkedIn, subscribe to our weekly newsletter, and join in with others in our Scaling community…

- https://www.linkedin.com/in/stephen-adele/
- https://www.linkedin.com/in/zachery-lewis-will/
- https://readyforscaling.com/products
- https://www.linkedin.com/company/readyforscaling/

Acknowledgments

It's with immense gratitude that Zach and I acknowledge the many people in our lives who helped inspire and shape this book.

Gratitude From Stephen Adelé

First and foremost, I would like to acknowledge Charles Dhanaraj. While teaching at the University of Denver Daniels College of Business, you served as our initial inspiration, encouraging Zach and me to embark on this journey of putting our ideas into writing a book and helping us come up with the title. Your influence has been a guiding light.

To my business partner, Zach, this book is as much yours as it is mine. Your willingness to listen to countless stories and business lessons, your battle-tested wisdom, and your contributions throughout these pages have been invaluable. And, the development and refinement of our scaling tools would not have been possible without your dedication and partnership.

To my family—my wife, who is my best friend, soulmate, and un-wavering supporter of every crazy idea I have; and my children, who I will forever remain their number one fan… Your perspectives and how you describe me to your friends are my ultimate measures of success.

A special thanks to my parents for always believing in me, supporting me, and giving me the space to let my entrepreneurial spirit thrive. Your faith in me has been the bedrock of my journey.

I am grateful to my peers and the prestigious faculty at the University of Denver, who helped crystallize many of the ideas and theories found throughout our consulting practice. Kerry Plemmons, Scott McLagan, Corey Ciocchetti, Josh Ross, Neil Pollard, Andy Cohen, Mike Broker, and David Swanger—your intellectual rigor and support have been instrumental.

To my co-founding partners at QuickBox (Chris, Nick, James, and Chad), you made our journey incredibly fun and rewarding. You were the absolute best team I could have hoped for, and our shared experiences have been a significant part of this book, and my life.

My three biggest mentors—Seth Yakatan, whose wisdom and calming presence have been invaluable; Todd Ordal, who has provided unparalleled leadership guidance as the world's best CEO coach; and Joel Appel, whose entrepreneurial insights on building lasting brands and legacies have guided me in every endeavor.

For the contributions made by fellow business founders—Ronak Shah (Obvi), Jake Karls (Mid-Day Squares), and Anwar Imani (Smashtech)—may you continue to find scaling success. Remember, I'm always rooting for you.

A heartfelt thanks to Jeremiah O'Brian for lifting me up during times of writer's block and sparking new light in my quest to write. Your encouragement has meant more than you'll ever know.

Lastly, to our editor, Sue Mosebar, whom I've had the pleasure and privilege of working side by side with for over 20 years. I'm pretty sure we've written more words together than a collection of encyclopedias, and I'm not joking. Your meticulous eye and unwavering dedication have brought this book to life.

To all of you, my fellow entrepreneurs, business owners, and trailblazers, my deepest gratitude. This book would not have been possible without your support, encouragement, and belief in our vision.

~

Gratitude From Zach Lewis

Following Stephen's heartfelt acknowledgments, I would also like to
express my deep gratitude to everyone who has been part of this incredible journey. While Stephen has acknowledged many of the remarkable individuals who have influenced both of us, I want to highlight a few people who have specifically shaped my life and contributed to the completion of this book.

A profound thank you to my business partner, Stephen Adelé. Your wisdom, experience, and collaborative spirit have been invaluable throughout this process. Together, we have built something truly special, and I am excited for what the future holds.

To Sue Keeley, my partner, thank you for your unwavering support, perspective, and encouragement. You have been a pillar of strength and a source of inspiration, especially through the most challenging year of my life. Your belief in me and our journey has made all the difference.

To my son Tommy, you are a boundless source of inspiration. The time I spend with you is both rejuvenating and enlightening. Your laughter, curiosity, and spirit remind me of what truly matters. My greatest hope is that you grow up proud of me as your father.

To my good friends Eric Buttolph, Erik Van Buren, Josh Vriens, Will Leer, and my cousin Chris Lint, who have stood by me through thick and thin, challenging me when necessary and inspiring me to grow intellectually, emotionally, and spiritually. The world would be a better place with more men like you in it. Your unwavering friendship and support have been crucial in my journey, and I am deeply grateful for each of you.

To my parents, thank you for instilling in me a bias toward action and the courage to lean in and tackle the hard things. Your teachings on discipline, integrity, and the importance of fighting for what is right have been my guiding principles.

To my grandparents Carl and Marilyn, thank you for the warmth and light of your unwavering love. My life would've been a much darker place without it. My Papa Carl was a self-made businessman before the term entrepreneur was widely used. Your example and support have been a guiding light in my life, and I carry your lessons with me every day.

To the University of Denver's Executive MBA program and my Co-hort 78, thank you for being part of a truly transformational period in my life. Your insights, support, and camaraderie sharpened my skills and eased my challenging transition from military to civilian life. Our shared journey and the relationships formed during our time together were invaluable, and I am eternally grateful for the profound impact you have had on my journey.

To everyone who has supported and believed in our vision, my deep-est gratitude. This book would not have been possible without your encouragement and unwavering belief in our mission.

About the Authors

Stephen Adelé

In the illustrious world of entrepreneurship, some individuals stand out not just for the businesses they create but for the ethos they embody. Stephen Adelé is one such luminary, with a career that reads like a masterclass in business acumen and achievements. His journey is both awe-inspiring and deeply rooted in a genuine and passionate care for others' success.

Living in Denver, Colorado, Stephen provides strategic advisory services through his firm, Ready for Scaling. He is an Adjunct Professor at the University of Denver Daniels College of Business, where he teaches graduate and undergraduate courses on scaling new ventures and business strategy. His extensive experience and commitment to education make him a respected figure among aspiring entrepreneurs and business leaders.

Stephen's entrepreneurial repertoire is just as impressive, encompassing diverse roles that highlight his versatility. From real estate ventures to board memberships to leading companies as the CEO, his journey is a rich tapestry of experiences. He has successfully started, built, and scaled multiple companies through self-funding, public markets, and private equity, including his latest venture, QuickBox Fulfillment, which he led to over $100 million in revenue in less than five years.

His accolades include being a three-time finalist for EY's prestigious Entrepreneur of the Year Award (2006, 2007, 2021) and earning three consecutive Inc. 500 Awards for America's fastest-growing private companies (2019, 2020, 2021). Additionally, he was a finalist for Best Boss in America and is a sought-after guest lecturer at entrepreneurial conferences and business schools.

Stephen's approach synthesizes the pragmatism of a seasoned entrepreneur with the heart of a mentor, guiding others through the intricacies of business with wisdom and wit. His story is one of inspiration, showcasing a visionary who has walked the path, charted the challenges, and emerged with both success and his soul intact. For Stephen, it's not just about accolades; it's about creating legacies and helping the next generation of leaders achieve their own success.

Zach Lewis

Zach Lewis stands as a testament to modern entrepreneurship, embodying the essence of ethical leadership, creative problem-solving, and strategic growth. His diverse career spans government, military, corporate, academic, and startup environments, showcasing a versatile skill set and an unyielding commitment to excellence.

As a veteran of the U.S. Navy SEALs, Zach has navigated some of the most challenging and high-pressure situations imaginable. This experience has ingrained in him a profound understanding of operational leadership and strategic planning, which he now leverages in the business world. His educational background, capped with an Executive MBA from the Daniels College of Business at the University of Denver, complements his practical experience, providing a solid foundation in business theory and application.

In the entrepreneurial arena, Zach founded Parka Products, a consumer electronics company, which represented his innovative spirit and resilience in such a competitive industry. Now, as a co-founding member at Ready for Scaling, Zach and Stephen partner with businesses to identify and overcome the constraints that hinder their growth, applying his unique blend of military precision and business acumen.

Zach's leadership philosophy is rooted in empathy, vulnerability, and action-orientation. He believes in creating cultures where every team member feels valued and empowered, fostering environments that encourage continual development and maximum impact. His commitment to social and environmental causes, along with his advocacy for open communication and accountability, highlights his truly holistic approach to leadership.

Zach Lewis's story is one of resilience, innovation, and unwavering dedication to creating positive change. His work continues to inspire and mentor the next generation of leaders, embodying the spirit of entrepreneurship and the relentless pursuit of excellence.

Made in United States
Orlando, FL
30 October 2024